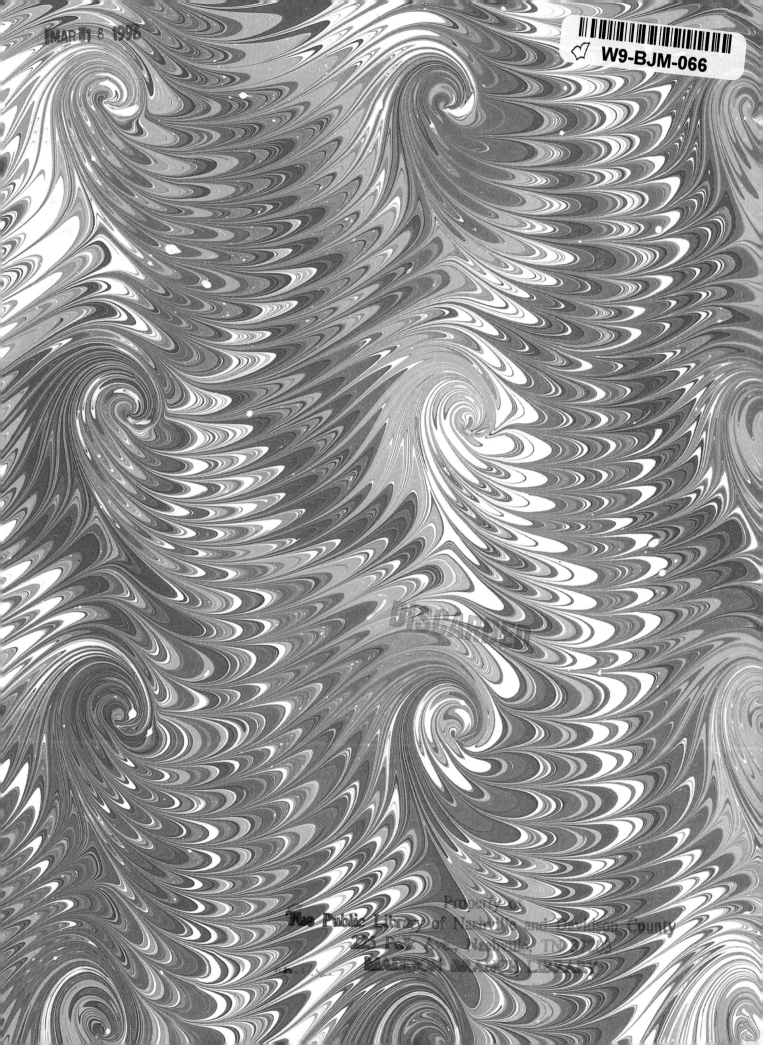

WATERFOWL PAINTING
Blue Ribbon Techniques
by William Veasey

Schiffer Publishing Ltd

Box E, Exton, Pennsylvania 19341

Other books by the author:

Waterfowl Carving, Blue Ribbon Techniques, with Cary Hull
Bills and Feet: An Artisan's Handbook, with Sina Kurman
Blue Ribbon Pattern Series:
        Book I - Full Size Decorative Decoy Patterns
        Book II - Miniature Decoy Patterns
        Book III - Head Patterns
        Book IV - Song Bird Patterns
        Book V - Shore Bird Patterns
        Book VI - Miniature Decorative Patterns
        Book VII - Hunting Bird Patterns
        Book VIII - Birds of Prey Patterns

Forthcoming books:

Upland Game Bird Patterns
Reproduction of Antique Decoys
Blue Ribbon Burning Techniques

Copyright © 1983 by William Veasey
Library of Congress Catalog Number: 83—61645

Printed in the United States of America.
ISBN: 0-916838-90-0
Published by Schiffer Publishing Ltd., 1469 Morstein Road, West Chester, Pennsylvania 19380

DEDICATION

For my father
William Wright Veasey
whose great gift to me was the
idea of commitment and excellence

ACKNOWLEDGEMENTS

Photography: Tricia Veasey

Art Work: Sina "Pat" Kurman

I would like to give special recognition to Bob Biddle, Nan Furness, Pat Biddle, Jim Fisher, Doug Eppes, Debra Norvell, Sina "Pat" Kurman, Ned Mayne, Ned Ewell, George Walker, John Garton, Bobby Kerr and Armand Carey, Carl Addison, and Jay Polite for their invaluable conversations over the years in regard to color. It was through these conversations and exchanges that I was able to come to some knowledge and understanding in the use of color in a simplified manner which could be a beginning place for carvers and painters. Each of these people mentioned and others have in the course of our individual relationships contributed greatly to my growth.

During the preparation of this book many other areas had to suffer, I would like to thank my family, Dotty, Roxayne, Darcy and Michael for taking up the slack and maintaining equilibrium.

I would also like to thank the following carvers for the use of their carvings in the preparation of this book: Jack Alderson, Tom Birch, E.J. Ham, Sina "Pat" Kurman, Penny Macy, Debra Norvell, Sandy Stromberg, Paul Suarez, Ralph Moffett and Harry Groome.

William Veasey

Table of Contents

INTRODUCTION 7
WORDS OF WISDOM 9
A COLORFUL HISTORY 11
BRUSHES AND PAINT 13
PAINTING INSTRUCTIONS BY SPECIES 17
    Brant 17
    Canada goose 21
    Canada Goose 21
    White Fronted Goose 25
    Blue Goose 26
    Richardson's Goose 26
    Swan 27
    Black Duck 30
    Gadwall 34
    Mallard 41
    Pintail 51
    Shoveler 60
    Blue Winged Teal 64
    Cinnamon Teal 71
    Green Winged Teal 77
    American Widgeon 87
    Wood Duck 89
    Bufflehead 96
    Canvasback 102
    Common Loon 110
    American Golden Eye 112
    Barrow's Golden Eye 112
    Hooded Merganser 119
    Red-Breasted Merganser 126
    American Merganser 131
    Ring Necked Duck 134
    Old Squaw 139
    Red Head 143
    Ruddy Duck 150
    Lesser Scaup 155
    Greater Scaup 155
HUNTING DECOYS ....
    Ring Necked Duck 160
    Pintail 161
    Canvasback 162
    Green Winged Teal 164
    Blue Winged Teal 166
BILLS ....
    American Merganser 167
    Hooded Merganser 167
    Mallard 168
    Black Duck 168
    Baldpate 169
    Gadwall 169
    Pintail 170
    Shoveler 170
    Blue Winged Teal 171

Bills continued:

Cinnamon Teal 171
Green Winged Teal 172
Wood Duck 172
Lesser Scaup 173
Greater Scaup 173
American Goldeneye 174
Barrow's Goldeneye 174
Canvasback 175
Bufflehead 175
Canada Goose 176
Brant 176
White Fronted Goose 176
Snow or Blue Goose 176
Harlequin 177
Old Squaw 177
Red Head 180
Ring Necked Duck 180
Red Breasted Merganser 181

AIR BRUSH TECHNIQUE 184
VERMICULATIONS 189
UNUSUAL STUDIES

Snow Goose 194
White Fronted Goose 195
Whistling Swan 196
Canada Goose 197
American Goldeneye 198
Barrow's Goldeneye 200
Canvasback 201
Hooded Merganser 202
Cinnamon Teal 203
Blue Winged Teal 204
American Eider Drake 205
Fulvous Tree or Whistling Duck 207
Mandarin Duck 207
Red Head 208
Pintail 210
Green Winged Teal 211
Ring Necked Duck 212
Scaup 213
Ruddy Duck 214
Shoveler 216
Mallard 217
Widgeon 218
Wood Duck 220
Gadwall 221

SOURCE BOOKS 222
INDEX 223

Introduction

One day, soon after the publication of *Waterfowl Carving, Blue Ribbon Techniques,* I was visiting my publisher and in well designed spontaneity he asked if I thought anyone would ever be able to do a good book on color and painting. My answer, of course was "no". There are too many variables, and I proceeded to list a few. Each of us percieves color differently, color of birds vary to a great degree, geographically, chronologically, individually (within species). The color varies in different stages of moult. Paint color varies greatly from manufacturer to manufacturer, the color also varies from batch to batch from the same manufacturer. Color varies under different light sources.

Fortunately my publisher in his own subtle way ignored my considerations and gave me the assignment to "think about it", this meant that "the book was on". Having made this decision he would not let me not think about it. Frequent calls to see where "we" were in regard to "our" project led to an acceptance on my part to really begin the agonizing process of doing another major book.

I find it a great deal easier to instruct by "show and tell", than by writing. Once it is written I must then go over and over to insure that what is written is actually what I intended to convey, I have not yet developed a method of writing a "shrug of the shoulders" or the "raising of an eyebrow".

Certainly we know the needs of beginning carvers and painters. It is these needs through which we developed the techniques that work for everyone, and, that is not to say that these are the only techniques. I am quite certain that there are countless other techniques which would work just as well; there are also others which work *most of the time,* these we have rejected for beginners because we have developed simple straight forward techniques which work for everyone, everytime. It is then the responsibility of the individual student to seek out other techniques, further refinement and extentions of the basics which we offer here. Part of the process which we set forth here is the selection and use of color combinations to get to the same or relatively the same point. What we have done here is to use the simplest, most direct method of color selection closest to raw tube color. Later in your development we suggest you start "seeing" and using the various reds, greens and blues which show up in many areas. First master the simple and highly successful methods we set forth here. As to shadows and shading by all means you should develop these techniques. However, initially allow the contours and texturing of your sculpture do this for you then as you develop you may then employ more sophisticated techniques.

When you write something you can be sure of one thing, that somewhere, sometime it will come back to haunt you. What I am about to relate is one of the beautiful experiences which I welcome back anytime.

During the past few years I have offered a number of three day carving and painting seminars around the country. It started in Camden, South Carolina at The Kershaw County Vocational Center. E. J. Ham, commercial art teacher and carver invited me to do a three day seminar at the school. After clearing this with the administrator, Dr. Gil Wollard we made plans to do one in Jaunary 1982.

It was my intention to do one seminar, however before we even got started many people were asking what we would do "next" time. This began a series. By January 1983 this group had progressed in knowledge as well as the development of basic skills. Most of them were now aware of the competition shows and were showing signs of wanting to participate.

To make a long story much shorter we decided to conduct two weekend seminars one month apart, one for carving, one for painting, with texturing in between. Under this supervised situation the results are as follows, twenty participants (three absolute first time carvers) six shows, won 94 ribbons including many blue and several best of category.

What we did there was to basically employ the techniques outlined in *Waterfowl Carving, Blue Ribbon Techniques* for the carving seminar and the techniques outlined in this book *Waterfowl Painting, Blue Ribbon Techniques* for the painting seminar. My staff and I supervised and gave reinforcement to the group. We have since conducted many other seminars in South Carolina and plan several in Alabama, Georgia and North Carolina as well as Pennsylvania, New Jersey and anywhere else a few people are willing to listen.

It is not my intention in the preparation of this book to "paint the bird for you". It is rather my intention to give you the tools with which to work so that with what is presented here you may progress at your own pace and go as far as you want or need to go. This is the beginning, the spring board from which you may propel yourself to wherever you want to go. The basic tools are here, use them, add to them, replace them, and make them work for you.

Go for the Blue!

Words of Wisdom

Eldridge Arnold—When carving, burning and painting a bird sometimes it's not what you put in—it's what you leave out.

Knute R. Bartrug—Painting for the beginner is a study in patience. You must learn your colors, you must experiment with your colors, you must allow sufficient time and research for your technique to unfold. You cannot rush the process of becoming, not imposing your will for whatever reasons on it so as to require it to come to *your* schedule. So its pretty obvious that patience, research, practice and more practice be your guidlines.

Your brush can become a magician's wand, it can cover up carving mistakes and dazzle the public's eye... If all your guidlines are met, but like a magician that doesn't practice, you could turn your carving into an ugly duckling.

I am not sold on acrylics I love their effect, their drying time and the need not to have to concentrate on other carvings while this one is drying. But I want todays carvings to last the life of the old masters oil paintings, to be timeless works of art. No one knows the life of acrylics so until they do I will not approve them for this art form.

Armand Carey—First thing you want is a good gesso base. Then you need good brushes, #8 red sable for the feathering and a one inch wash brush for your base colors. Look at the lightest color on the duck. Mix your paint to match that color very, very thin. Paint the whole duck that color, then add your base dark colors where needed, make sure paints are well watered down, thin. Now you are ready to paint your details.

Take #8 brush, squish it down, and do feathers. Each has 4 — 5 coats paint with a wash of color desired between each coat. Practice makes perfect. You can use an old board to practice your feathers on. All my feathers are white then darkened to color I want. I work from tail to head.

Ned Ewell—I am a firm believer in trial and error, determination and the desire to get better. Never be satisfied with what you have done, everyday you work on your project, you learn. After you have finished your work, even if it really looks good, say to yourself I can do better, then get right up and do it.

Don't try to work on too many projects at one time, spend as much time on each project that you can. Study your birds in their natural habitat whenever possible.

Nan Furness—Think in terms of learning to "see" color as opposed to learning to "mix" color. It is necessary to see the componets of a color and to feel it's character (wet, cool, warm, dry, etc.).

People planning to begin painting invariably ask for formulas for mixing. A brief exercise using primaries with white and perhaps black can usually end the preoccupation with formula.

Color is determined largely by light source and action and interaction of surrounding color. These effects are part of "seeing color". However, much time with trial and error can be eliminated by a brief demonstration of what color does on paper or wood, for example: color can recede or advance, it can soften or sharpen, shadows can settle, and lighting can float.

Most important, try it. See what it does for you. Choose your equipment to serve you. Perfect equipment is as much an illusion as the mixing formula. Use what is comfortable in your hands to create what you are now able to see.

William Hazzard—I feel each artist should strive to get the depth colors in each feather, using acrylic paints. I put a burnt umber wash over burning on feathers, then put my depth colors on. Painting on most obvious colors last.

Cliff Hollestelle—Color wheels, basic knowledge of mixing colors, and reference books can be most helpful with painting; but nothing can take the place of working with the medium you have selected (oil and acrylics). Trial and error can help you gain a better understanding of what the paint can do for you. The more you paint the more you will learn the potential and limitations of the medium.

As I paint, using acrylics, I first seal the wood surface using two coats of sealer. After the decoy is fully dried, I coat the piece using a base color—generally burnt umber—followed by washes of various colors to emulate the living bird. These layers of paint usually consist of more water than paint and, as you might guess, you will paint and repaint the wooden sculpture many, many times.

Painting can be an enjoyable experience by learning its strengths and weaknesses.

Penny Miller—Painting is as much attitude as anything else. It is alright to strive for perfection, but it is very important to recognize, and be happy with every little improvement you make.

Jim Sprankle—The end result of any carving will be how well it was painted. Pre-plan the painting of any carving, this should be done as you are carving the bird.

Above all, take your time, don't hurry. Remember there are no short cuts or easy way in this business of carving decorative birds.

Robert Sutton—Do a lot of research and feel sure in your own mind that you know what the bird looks like. With this knowledge you will carve and paint a much better bird.

Jimmie Vizier—Regardless of the technique and type of paint used by a wildfowl painter it is important to achieve softness while retaining the brilliance of color.

Joe Wooster—The most common mistake that I see as a judge of the carving contests is a complete lack of knowledge about color. Beginning carvers should realize that to be successful in wildfowl carving they must research the science of color as thoroughly as the art of carving, on the birds they hope to glorify.

Painting wildfowl carving is no different then any other form of painting, it helps like hell to know what you are trying to do.

A Colorful History

It was 1832, Victoria would soon ascend to the throne of England with her beloved Albert. Constable was at the pinnacle of his career. Brighton was the fashionable resort. The Victorian Age was about to begin. Two eager young men, William Winsor and Henry Newton, met, talked and decided that supplying artists with colours would be a profitable and worthwhile enterprise and also marry their respective interests in painting and science.

It was no accident that they established their firm Winsor & Newton at 38 Rathbone Place, just north of Oxford Street and that Bohemian part of London later called Fitrovia, where a number of eminent painters and sculptors, including Constable already had their studios.

The young firm's initial success was due in no small measure to Winsor's technical expertise. It was he who realized that the moisture-retaining properties of glycerine could be utilized to manufacture water colours in pans which were much simpler and more convenient to use than dry water colour cakes.

These early moist water colours enjoyed a well deserved popularity and when in 1837, the year of Queen Victoria's accession, Winsor & Newton introduced Chinese White, a particularity opaque form of zinc white, the success of Winsor & Newton was assured.

The enterprising young partners soon saw that there were many other opportunities apart from water colours. For instance, Winsor's inventions lead him to introduce and patent glass syringes as oil colour containers, a distinct impovement on the traditional skin bladders which artists had used until then.

This development was closely followed in 1841 by the manufacture of collapsible metal tubes for artist's colours which became as much a symbol of the artist as his palette, and are still used today. Because of their convenience they were readily accepted and later used for water colours as well.

To cope with demand, the partners acquired workshops at Blackfriars and at Kings Cross, but very soon afterwards in 1844, increasing sales required that they commission an entirely new, purpose-built factory, with the latest steampowered engines, in Kentish Town.

The most famous of English colour makers at this time was George Field. He specialized in cake pigments and was renowned for his perfectionism in the quest, for maximum purity and permanence in all artist's pigments.

Naturally enough, Winsor & Newton, who completely identified with the same ideals of technical excellance, purchased pigments from the master of English Colourists. They were the first artist's colourmen to actually publish the composition and permanence of their colours.

Recognition of this emphasis on quality came fast. As early as 1841 they were granted the Royal Warrant. Queen Victoria, herself a keen amateur painter, appointed Winsor & Newton as her artist's colourmen. This was but the first of many such Royal appointments.

In 1851, the only prize medal open to competitors in the field of artist's colours at the Great Exhibition was awarded to Winsor & Newton. This accolade was repeated at the Great International Exhibition of 1867.

William Winsor died in 1865 and his share in the firm was inherited by his son. When he died in 1879, Henry Newton purchased his late partner's share. And then, a few months before his own death in 1882, Newton sold the business to the newly incorporated firm of Winsor & Newton Limited which included members of both families among its shareholders.

In the nineteenth century, England was the workshop of the world and Winsor & Newton's reputation for quality resulted in its products being exported all over the world.

Sales to the United States of America began in the 1860's. In 1893 the firm won three awards at the World Columbian Exhibition in Chicago, and the following year Winsor & Newton set up its own New York office.

The United States quickly developed into the firm's biggest overseas market, and in 1915 the American subsidiary company was incorporated.

Today, agents and distributors have been appointed throughout the world, with over sixty-five percent of the company's production being exported.

Though the name of Winsor & Newton was synonymous with fine paints and pigments as long ago as 1911 the firm began to diversify into craft products and this change of approach, and consequent extra source of income, proved to have been a most farsighted decision when overseas markets contracted during the 1920's.

The depression years had serious consequences for Winsor & Newton which were countered by expansion into the manufacture and sale of student's colours. Winsor & Newton's Scholastic Range was launched in 1933. This line of colours is now known by the brand name London.

As the business grew, it became necessary to move premises again, this time to the pleasant London suburb of Wealdstone. All Winsor & Newton's activities were concentrated there, colour manufacturing was transferred from Kentish Town in 1938 and the administrative offices moved from Rathbone Place just before the outbreak of the Second World War in 1939.

Despite wartime raw material shortages the manufacture of artist's and draftsmen's colours continued apace. The firm's products proved to be a valuable foreign exchange earner in those critical years.

After the war, brush demand increased and in 1946 a new factory was opened at Lowestoft, the East Coast fishing port. Brushes are still made there as well as at Wealdstone.

Winsor & Newton expanded again in 1963 when the company acquired Charles G. Page Ltd., whose principal activity is the manufacture of children's paint boxes. Established in 1932, Charles G. Page Ltd. is based in Tottenham, North London.

In 1976 Winsor & Newton was acquired by the Reckett & Colman Group which assured continued expansion and service to the art world.

One hundred fifty years have seen many changes, but one thing as least remains the same, a wholehearted dedication to fine quality.

Remarkably, Winsor & Newton chemists still use some of the original formulae developed by the original partners. Indeed certain delicate pigments are still ground by hand in the way of the early colourmen. Few, if any, other firms still pay this scrupulous attention to detail.

At the same time a colour research program continues to apply these exacting standards to new techniques.

This then is the secret of Winsor & Newton's 150 year-long story. The marriage of the crafts and skills of the past with the best of today's technologies so as to place the finest quailty materials at the disposal of the craftsman and artist.

Brushes and Paints

BRUSHES

All Artist's brushes are pretty much alike, aren't they? A brush is a brush isn't it?

Believe that and you're headed for trouble.

There are many ways to skimp in the making of a brush. Ways that don't become evident until you're right in the middle of painting and a hair frays or falls out, or the brush fails to hold taper, or it grows "lazy" and loses resiliency.

Many great artists today use the Series 7 Sable brush. Little do they know, the brush was originally designed for Queen Victoria by Winsor & Newton in approximately 1841, at a cost that would be expensive even at todays prices. The brush is still one of the finest made and is in large demand.

Show a master brushmaker a tuft of red sable and he can tell you what kind of animal it came from, whether it was male or female, or if it came from a frigid or moderate climate.

Why does it matter? Because there's a vast difference in how it will perform for you.

Mink, for example, makes a nice fur coat but a poor sable brush. The North Asian kolinsky produces the finest red sable in the world, and the very best kolinsky hair comes from the tail of a male. This is the hair that is used exclusively in top-of-the-line red sable brushes.

The Seamless Story

Like stockings, the best ferrules are seamless.

Seams tend to pull apart with use. Paint and thinner can work their way up inside the ferrule and play havoc, and the ferrule may begin to wobble. That's why great artists' brushes use only seamless ferrules. They cost a few cents more, but if you have ever cursed a wobbly brush, you'll know it's worth it.

Getting A Better Handle

Even handles are special. They should be shaped from selected New England birch to achieve the best balance in your hand. The pores should be sealed to prevent cracking and triple lacquer on them for long life. The handle should be cemented in the ferrule so it won't loosen.

THE CARE OF BRUSHES

Good, well kept brushes will not in themselves produce good painting but they will have a much longer life and be far more pleasant to work with if these very simple rules are followed.

Always clean your brushes immediately after use

Never leave them resting on their bristles or hairs

Do not leave bristles or hairs submerged or soaking in water

Shape up hairs after cleaning

If you are storing brushes away for any length of time, make sure they are clean and perfectly dry before putting them away in a box with a tight fitting lid. If the brushes are not absolutely dry, they will develope mildew: if the closure is not secure, they may be damaged by moths.Mothballs or naphthalene may be used as a moth deterrent, but neither should be relied upon as a sure preventative.

Oils and Alkyds

To clean Oil or Alkyd paint from your brushes, rinse them in Mineral Spirit to remove surface paint, the shake the Mineral Spirit from the brush and hold it under cool running water. Next, rub the bristle gently on a cake of ordinary soap, work up a lather on the palm of your hand and rinse the brush again in cool water. Do this until there is no trace of color in the lather. Then give the brush a final rinse and ensure that all traces of soap are removed. Shake out the water from the bristles, shape up the brush and rest it in a pot or jar, bristles uppermost and free from contact with any surface.

Paint should never be allowed to dry on any brush. Should this happen, they may be treated with brush cleaning solutions manufactured for this purposes, the normal cleaning procedure should then be followed.

Water Colors   Follow the same procedure as above, but using soap and water only. It is not necessary to rinse the brushes in Mineral Spirit first.

Acrylics

Brushes that have been used in Acrylic colors must be throughly washed with cool water immediately after use. Follow the procedure for oil color brushes using household soap only. It is not necessary to rinse brushes in Mineral Spirits. Never use hot water as it may make the paint coagulate. Avoid the use of detergent instead of soap. When the brushes are dry, store them away as with oil brushes if you will not be using them again for some time.

Acrylic colors and media should not be allowed to dry on brushes or other painting equipment, but if this does happen they may be treated with brush cleaning solutions manufactured for this purpose.

Synthetic Brushes

Synthetic fibers require similar care to that required by natural hair. Oil and Alkyd brushes should be rinsed in Mineral Spirit, then cleaned with household soap and water. Water Color and Acrylic brushes should be cleaned with ordinary soap and cool water. Should the brush begin to lose its shape and the fibers droop, simply soak the brush in hot, but not boiling, water for 1-2 minutes, shape up the brush and store in a pot or jar, fibers uppermost.

Red Sable

Red sable comes from weasel and Kolinsky tails, both commonly grouped under the name red tarter marten. To get the finest quality red sable, only the best hair from the tails is selected. A top quality red sable brush must have the finest quality hair: uniform in length, strength, thickness and elasticity (spring). It is expensive but makes the very best brush.

Ox Hair

The ox hair used in brushes is taken from the ears of oxen, and comes in many qualities. It has great tensile strength, and does not break off under strenuous use in any kind of color. The finest grade is the short, natural hair from oxen of the Swiss Alps and a few other mountainous regions of the world. This hair is light, rather blonde in color, and although short, has a relatively long-tapered point. Some breeds of oxen have hair of a long, tapered,

springy character which has excellent properties when used in any type of color. Dark ox hair varies more in quality.

Camel Hair

The phrase "camel hair" when applied to brushes, does not indicate hair from a camel. Camel hair is a trade term, the finer grades of which are squirrel hair, while other grades are pony and goat hair.

Camel hair brushes are used for an extremely wide range of services: watercolor and tempera painting, washes, renderings with ink, as dusters and mops in easel painting; for lacquering, touch-up, and marking; and lettering brushes and quills.

The making of a brush from camel hair requires almost at much skill as for red sable, ox

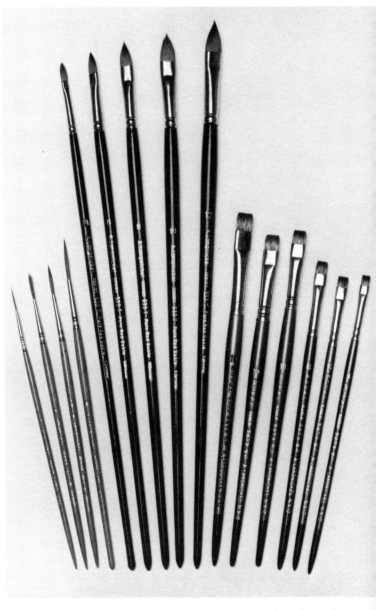

Example of line of very fine Langnickle brushes through Beebe Hooper, Chula Vista, California

Example of assortment of Grumbacher and Robert Simmons brushes available through Veasey Studios, 955 Blue Ball Road, Elkton, Maryland 21921

hair, bristle, or any other hair, and as much care must also be taken in the selection of hair in order to produce brushes of consistently excellant quality.

Bristle

Bristle for artist's brushes is selected and specially dressed. It is obtained only from hogs and boars of the Far East. Hair and bristle are not similar. These are the important differences:

1. Hair has a single, individual, natural point, while bristle has multiple natural tips (flags).
2. Bristle has a unique taper not found in other brushmaking material.
3. Natural hair is not uniform in diameter over its length. Red sable for example, is thicker in the mid-portion, called the "belly", than at the ends. The "butt" or base of the hair is the end opposite the tip. Red sable tapers to a fine point, whereas bristle has the multiple tip (flag) and the diameter of the bristle increases to the butt.

Synthetic Hair Brushes

When budgets don't permit the purchase of quality hair or bristle brushes, synthetic hair brushes provide an excellant substitute. The nylon filaments in the brush head range from very fine for watercolors to thick for acrylics and oil. Synthetic hair brushes are available as rounds, flats, and brights in a variety of sizes.

Brush Buying Tips

1. Buy the best brush you can afford.
2. Most brush hair or bristle is dipped in a gum arabic solution (completely water soluble) before shipping to protect the shape of the brush. Before testing the quality of the brush, be sure to gently move the hair or bristle from side to side to remove the material.
3. Always wet brushes throughly (except bristle) to see how well they point or give you a sharp, chiseled edge. The "spring" or snap resilience can also be determined by wetting and applying pressure in the palm of your hand. Ask for a cup of water if none is available where brushes are displayed. This practice is quite common.

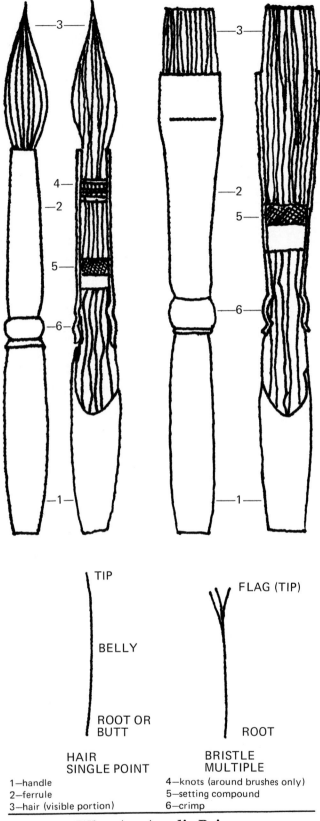

TIP

BELLY

ROOT OR
BUTT

HAIR
SINGLE POINT

FLAG (TIP)

ROOT

BRISTLE
MULTIPLE

1—handle
2—ferrule
3—hair (visible portion)

4—knots (around brushes only)
5—setting compound
6—crimp

What Are Acrylic Paints

Acrylics are water thinned, plastic based artists' paints and mediums. They are the most versatile and permanent material the artist has at his disposal today. Acrylics are the first new proven advance since the introduction of oil paints and have many advantages over traditional media.

Acrylics are emulsion paints, meaning the plastic resin is suspended as minute solid particles in water. When the water evaporates in drying, the paints become insoluble and are quite permanent. The surface of a dry acrylic painting can be washed with soap and water for cleaning without harm.

No toxic thinners or mediums are used in acrylic painting. The acrylics have minimal odors, produce no fumes to permeate the studio or house, and are non-flammable.

Acrylic mediums are permanently fixible and do not yellow with age.

They dry quickly, have no chemical drying action over a long period of time as does oil paint, and, therefore, result in the most permanent, stable and durable color and paint films available for the artist's use today.

Acrylics have the ability to reflect light from within the paint film, have the power of producing "inner light" that Early Masters prized so highly. This is the reason they first turned to oil colors and used translucent paints over colored grounds. Since any desired degree of translucency is easily accomplished with the acrylic mediums, a greater brillance and variety of color effect is possible than with traditional media.

Artists first turned to acrylics for permanency and because of the freedom with which they could be used. Rules that hampered creativity could be ignored and still produce lasting results. Now, because of the great versatility of acrylics the artist can duplicate almost any traditional technique from water color to sculpture and even go beyond the traditional with the new techniques not possible before.

MAJOR PAINT AND BRUSH COMPANIES

Grumbacher
460 West 34th Street
New York, New York 10001

Winsor & Newton
555 Winsor Drive
Secaucus, New Jersey 07094

Liquitex (Binney and Smith)
1100 Church Lane
P.O. Box 431
Easton, Pennsylvania 18042

Hunt (Speedball)
1405 Locust Street
Philadelphia, Pennsylvania 19102

Painting Instructions

Brant decorative decoy by Tom Birch

Brant decorative decoy head detail

Species: Brant
Sex: Drake and Hen

PAINTING INSTRUCTIONS

Color list: *Black, White, Burnt umber, Ultra-marine blue, Raw sienna.*

Head, Neck, Bill, and Chest, Rump, Primaries, Tail Feathers, and Feet: black, using ultra-marine blue and burnt umber to make the black.

Under Rump and band around the Tail: white with a touch of burnt umber.

Sides: undercoated with light tan, using burnt umber and white, edged with white, washed with white, and a final wash with burnt umber.

Back and Upper Wings: burnt umber with a touch of white, edged with raw sienna and white.

Tertials and Secondary Feathers: final wash: ultra-thin black.

Neck Markings: white, touch of burnt umber.

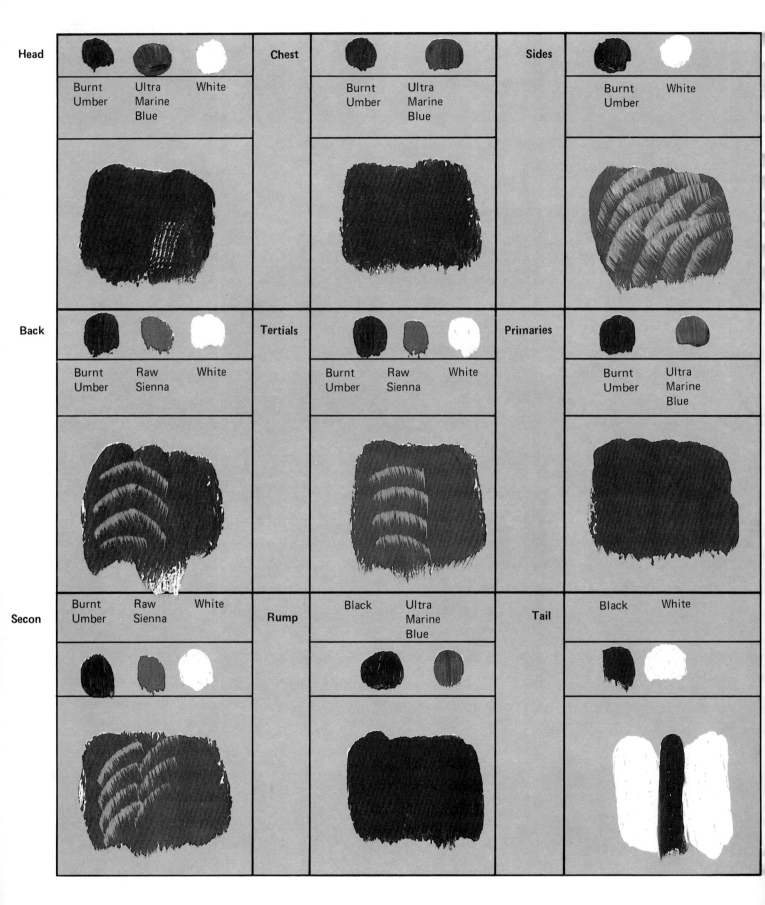

Head			Chest			Sides		
Burnt Umber	Ultra Marine Blue	White		Burnt Umber	Ultra Marine Blue		Burnt Umber	White

Back			Tertials			Primaries		
Burnt Umber	Raw Sienna	White		Burnt Umber	Raw Sienna	White		Burnt Umber	Ultra Marine Blue

Secon			Rump			Tail		
Burnt Umber	Raw Sienna	White		Black	Ultra Marine Blue		Black	White

18

Atlantic brant decoy — head and bill detail

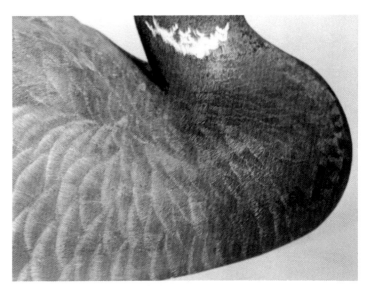

Atlantic brant decoy — chest and side detail

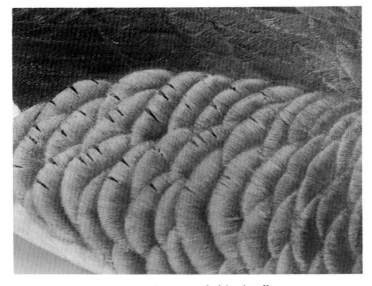

Atlantic brant decoy — close-up of side detail

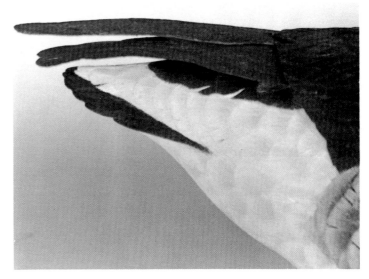

Atlantic brant decoy — tail and primaries

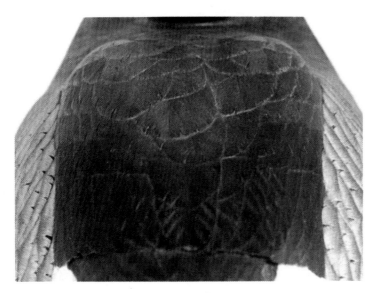

Atlantic brant decoy — back detail

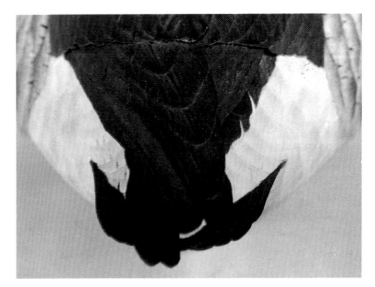

Atlantic brant decoy — primaries and tail area

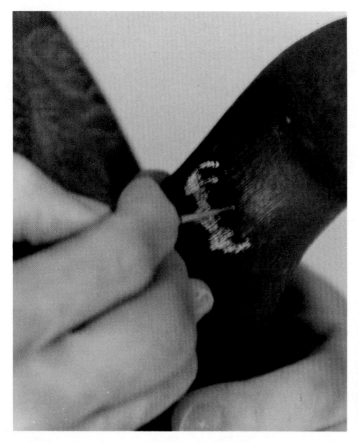

Atlantic brant decoy — final detail on neck

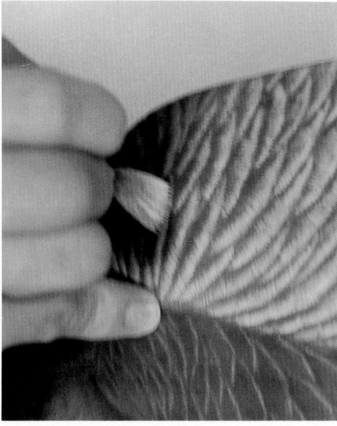

Atlantic brant decoy — edging side

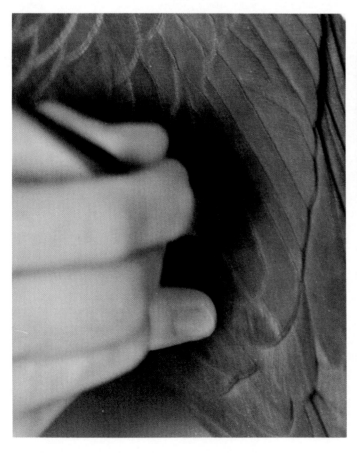

Atlantic brant decoy — stiple blending tertials

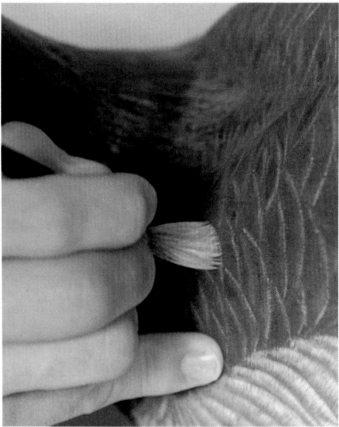

Atlantic brant decoy—edging back

Pair of canada geese

Canada goose — note position of neck

Canada goose resting

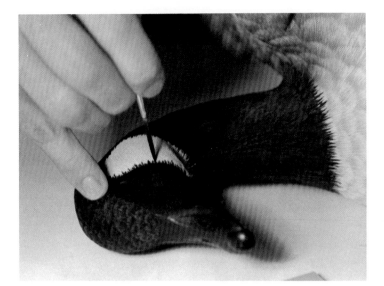

Goose — final edging on cheek patch

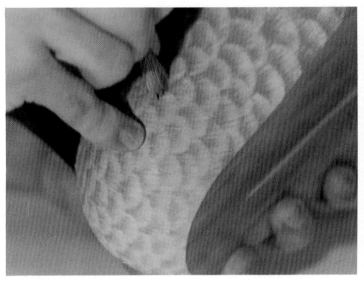

Goose — edging on chest

Goose — edging on secondary coverts

Goose — final edging on tail

Species: Canada Goose
Sex: Drake and Hen

PAINTING INSTRUCTIONS

Color list: *Black, White, Burnt umber, Raw sienna, Ultra-marine blue.*

Tail: black, burnt umber, and ultra-marine blue.

All Feathers: edged in white, washed with white several times, and final wash with burnt umber.

Trailing into the Rump: black, burnt umber, and ultra-marine blue.

Sides and Chest: **undercoat of tail**: pale tan, using white and burnt umber.

Upper Wings and Back: dark brown with burnt umber, touch of white. Edging with raw sienna and white, and washed with burnt umber.

Underside of the Wings: silvery-gray, using black, white, burnt umber.

Primary Feathers: brownish-black, using ultra-marine blue and burnt umber to make the black.

Neck, Head, Bill, Legs, and Feet: black, using ultra-marine blue and burnt umber to make the black. White patch on the cheek should have a faint touch of burnt umber in it.

CANADA GOOSE

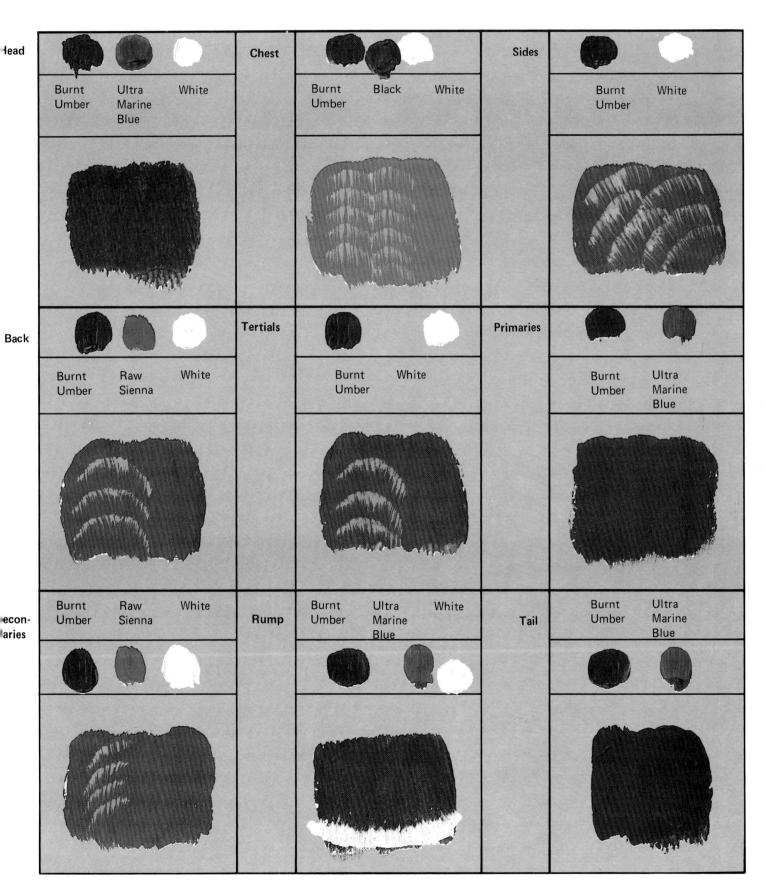

Head

Burnt Umber | Ultra Marine Blue | White

Chest

Burnt Umber | Black | White

Sides

Burnt Umber | White

Back

Burnt Umber | Raw Sienna | White

Tertials

Burnt Umber | White

Primaries

Burnt Umber | Ultra Marine Blue

Secondaries

Burnt Umber | Raw Sienna | White

Rump

Burnt Umber | Ultra Marine Blue | White

Tail

Burnt Umber | Ultra Marine Blue

Goose — edging sides

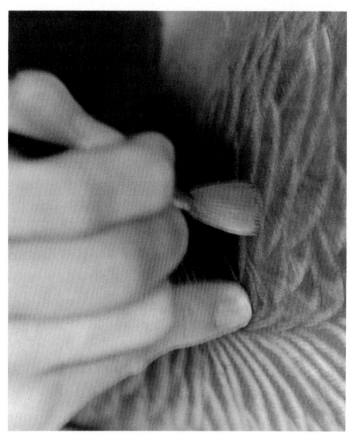

Goose — edging back

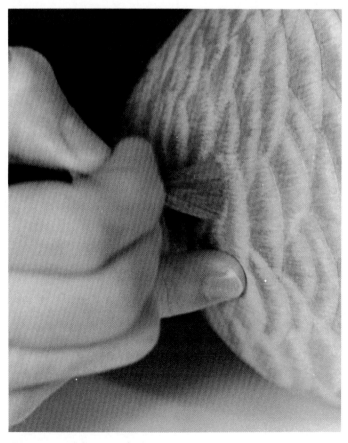

Goose — edging on chest

Goose — stiple blending on coverts

24

White fronted goose — note bill detail

Blue Goose — note position of tertials

Richardson Goose — note smaller size — shorter neck small head

Swan

Swan

Swan

Swan decorative decoy lifesize by Penny Mace — sealed ready to paint

Swan decorative decoy — after first few white edgings

Swan decorative decoy — after base washes with light tan

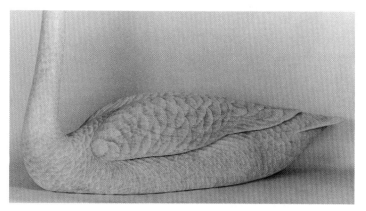

Swan decorative decoy after several washes and white edging

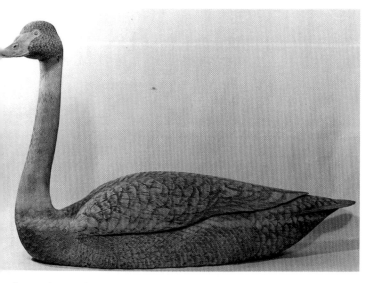

Swan decorative decoy after first light tan wash

Cygnet

Black duck decorative decoy — swimming position by Sina "Pat" Kurman

Black duck decorative decoy — head and bill detail

Black duck decorative decoy — front view bill detail

Species: Black Duck
Sex: Hen and Drake

PAINTING INSTRUCTIONS

Color list: *Black, Burnt umber, Ultra-marine blue, Yellow ochre, Cadmium red or Napthol crimson, Raw sienna, Thalo violet.*

Base Color for Body: best achieved by mixing burnt umber and ultra-marine blue. Starting with very little blue to keep the body brownish. It slowly darkens with successive washes, adding more ultra-marine blue as you go.

Tertials: same color with white added to lighten the center and the interior part of individual feathers. Edges are dark. All feathers' edges on the Black Duck are edged with raw sienna and a touch of white to make an orangish edging.

Secondaries: purplish, ranging from blue to purple. Use thalo violet and ultra-marine blue in mixture of softer, natural color—trailing faint edge of white. Faint edge of white does not occur on all black ducks.

Head Color: similar to a Mallard Hen. Base Color: white with raw sienna and a touch of burnt umber. A little more burnt umber than on the Mallard Hen. A little duskier.

Eyeline, Streaks, and Crown: mix brown umber with a black or brown umber with ultra-marine blue to gain intensity of color.

Nostrils: black.

Bill Color: varies widely from bright yellow to olive drab. The olive is mixed by using yellow ochre and black. Beware of getting it too dark; too olive. Often times the bill is mottled with black.

Feet: range from yellowish to reddish.

Nail. black.

BLACK DUCK

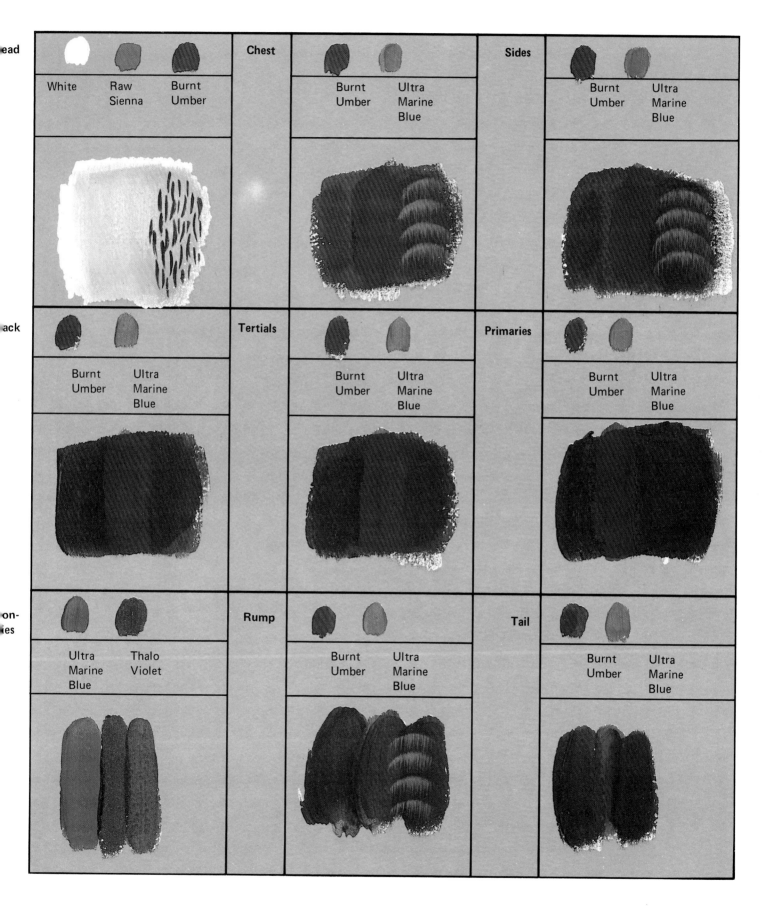

Head

White   Raw Sienna   Burnt Umber

Chest

Burnt Umber   Ultra Marine Blue

Sides

Burnt Umber   Ultra Marine Blue

Back

Burnt Umber   Ultra Marine Blue

Tertials

Burnt Umber   Ultra Marine Blue

Primaries

Burnt Umber   Ultra Marine Blue

Secon-daries

Ultra Marine Blue   Thalo Violet

Rump

Burnt Umber   Ultra Marine Blue

Tail

Burnt Umber   Ultra Marine Blue

Black duck decorative decoy — side detail

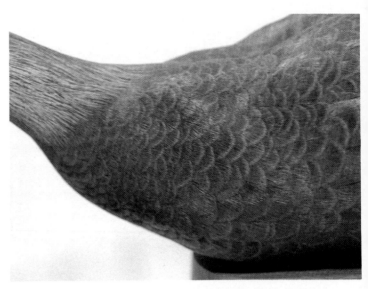

Black duck decorative decoy — neck and chest detail

Black duck — primary and tail detail

Black duck — top view of primary and tail detail

Black duck — head — cheek detail

Black duck—side detail, note iridescent patch

Black duck — front view bill detail

Black duck — crown detail

Black duck — secondaries area

Black duck — secondaries wing opened

Black duck — rump detail

Black duck — under wing detail

Pair of gadwalls

Gadwall drake — threatening position

Species: Gadwall
Sex: Drake

PAINTING INSTRUCTIONS

Color list: *Black, White, Burnt umber, Burnt sienna, Raw sienna, Red, Thalo violet.*
The entire body of the Gadwall Drake should be under-coated with a charcoal color, using black, white, and burnt umber to mix charcoal color. Then vermiculated with white. The chest feathers edged in white; reinforced several times.
Tail: gray, edged in white. Paint the tail tan, burnt umber, and white, edge with white, and wash with white several times to come out with a very soft gray.
Rump Area: black.
Scapulars: grayish, edged with white and washed with burnt sienna.
Tertial Feathers: gray, edged in white. The gray here is best achieved by mixing burnt umber and white, edged, then washed with white. Wing patch in front of the secondaries is thalo violet with traces of black.
Secondaries: white.
Primaries: brown, burnt umber. Darker on the edges, lighter in the interior of the feather.
Head Color: Base Color: raw sienna, white, and burnt umber to make a dark buffy color.
Dots and Streaks on the Head: also burnt umber with a touch of ultra-marine blue.
Eyeline, Crown, and back of the Neck: make burnt umber with a touch of black or ultra-marine blue.
Bill: black with a slight fleshy color along the edge of the upper and lower mandible, and sometimes small, black dots in that area.
Feet: yellow-orange.
Webs: blackish.

GADWALL DRAKE

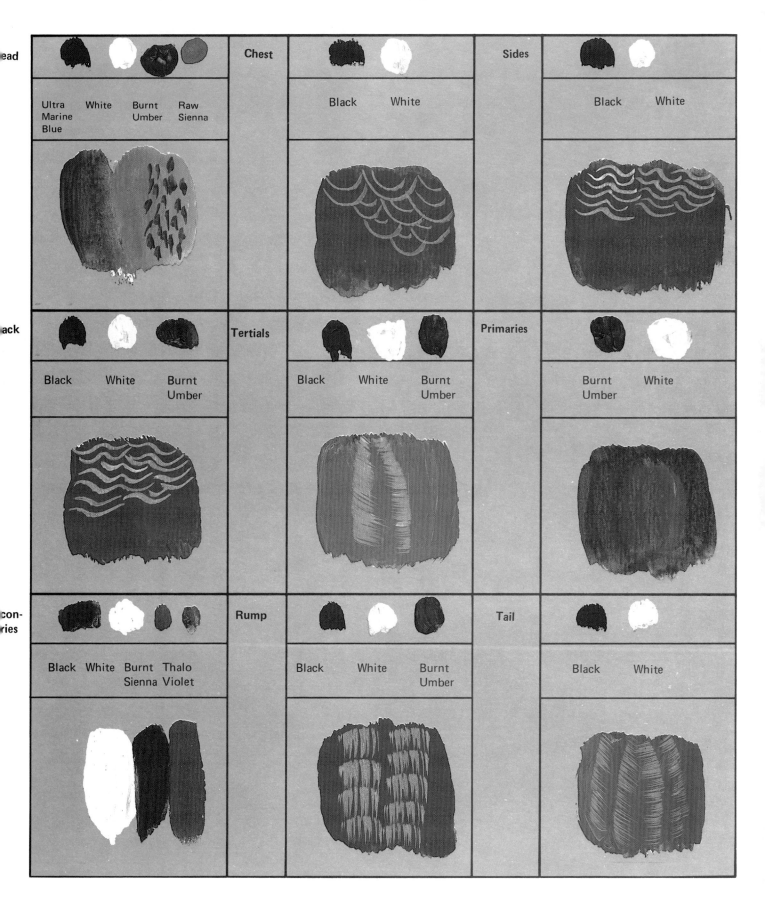

Head				Chest			Sides		
Ultra Marine Blue	White	Burnt Umber	Raw Sienna	Black	White		Black	White	

Back			Tertials				Primaries		
Black	White	Burnt Umber	Black	White	Burnt Umber		Burnt Umber	White	

Secondaries				Rump			Tail		
Black	White	Burnt Sienna	Thalo Violet	Black	White	Burnt Umber	Black	White	

Gadwall drake — wing detail

Gadwall drake — head detail

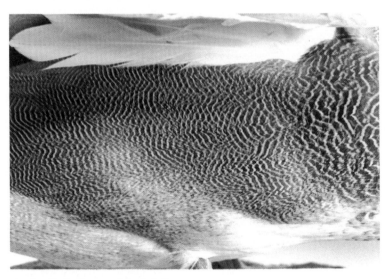

Gadwall drake — side detail

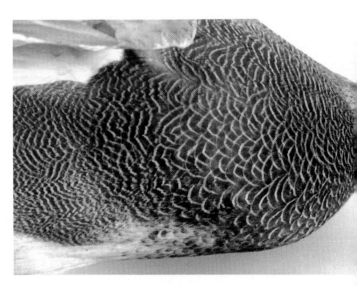

Gadwall drake — chest detail

Gadwall drake — tail area

Gadwall drake — rump area

Gadwall drake decoy — detailing tertial area

Gadwall drake decoy — detailing terial area

Gadwall drake decoy — detailing back

Gadwall drake decoy — detailing sides

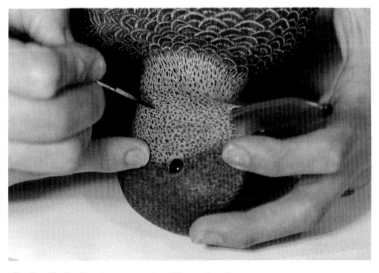

Gadwall drake decoy — detailing cheek

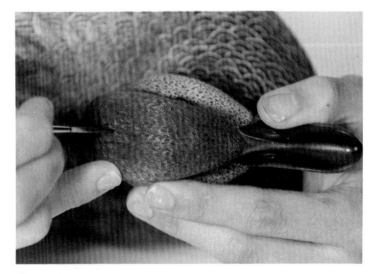

Gadwall drake decoy — detailing crown

Gadwall decoy by Tom Birch

Gadwall decoy—head detail

Gadwall—head

Gadwall—under wing

Gadwall—chest

Gadwall—wing

Gadwall—wing

Gadwall—tail

Gadwall drake — swimming

Gadwall drake — rump area

Gadwall drake — chest area

Gadwall drake — chest and side area

Gadwall drake — back and tail detail

Gadwall drake — swimming

Mallard hen — swimming position

Mallard hen decorative decoy by Jack Alderson

Species: Mallard
Sex: Hen

PAINTING INSTRUCTIONS

Color list: *Burnt umber, Raw sienna, White, Black, Yellow ochre, Napthol crimson or Cadmium red, Ultra-marine blue, Thalo violet.*

Base Color for Mallard Hen: burnt umber in successive washes. And for best results, add a touch of white to the burnt umber initially, so its successive washes do not get too dark, too quickly. After a soft sheem has developed, you may then begin edging all feather patterns and structures on the body of the hen, with raw sienna and white, blended to make a buffy to buffy orange color.

Secondaries: same as a drake: thalo violet, ultra-marine blue banded with two white bars and two black bars.

Primaries: burnt umber, touch of white, darker on the outside edges, lighter toward the center or near the shaft.

Base Head Color: white with raw sienna and a touch of burnt umber to make a dark buffy color. Eyeline is reinforced with burnt umber, touch of black. Also, all streaks and spots including crown and back of neck will be achieved with black and burnt umber to make a dark brown.

Bill Color: orange mottled with black or brown. The orange is made by mixing red and yellow ochre.

Feet: orange, reddish-orange.

41

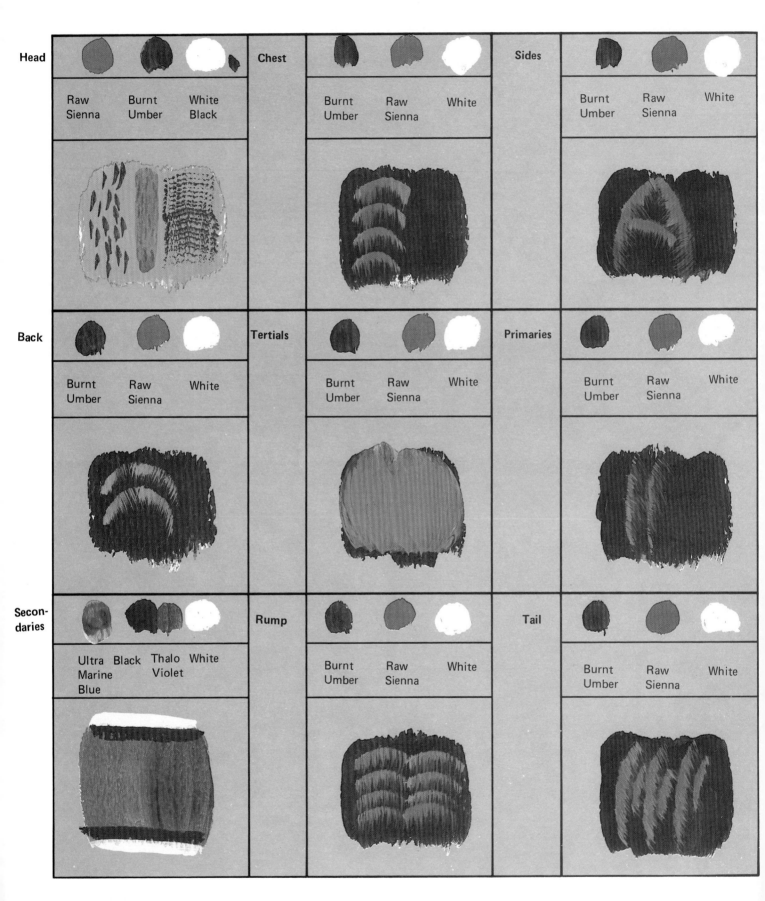

Head

Raw Sienna   Burnt Umber   White Black

Chest

Burnt Umber   Raw Sienna   White

Sides

Burnt Umber   Raw Sienna   White

Back

Burnt Umber   Raw Sienna   White

Tertials

Burnt Umber   Raw Sienna   White

Primaries

Burnt Umber   Raw Sienna   White

Secondaries

Ultra Marine Blue   Black   Thalo Violet   White

Rump

Burnt Umber   Raw Sienna   White

Tail

Burnt Umber   Raw Sienna   White

Mallard hen decorative decoy — head, bill and chest detail

Mallard hen decorative decoy — primary and tail detail

Mallard hen decorative decoy — cheek and bill detail

Mallard hen decorative decoy — primaries

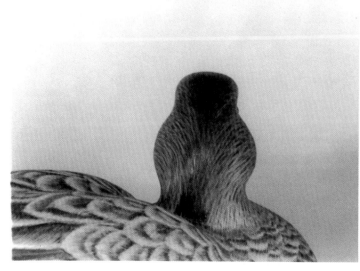

Mallard hen decorative decoy — crown detail

Mallard hen decorative decoy — primaries and tail detail

Mallard drake swimming

Mallard drake decorative decoy by Tom Birch

Species: Mallard
Sex: Drake

PAINTING INSTRUCTIONS

Color list: *Black, White, Burnt umber, Ultra-marine blue, Thalo green, Thalo yellow-green, Yellow ochre, Cadmium red or Napthol crimson, Burnt sienna.*
Tail and Underside: silvery-gray.
Undercoat the Upper Tail: a dusky gray, and then the tail feathers should be edged in white.

Under Rump: also gray with a white band bordering black under rump, which intersects in a line from secondaries, running through the vent area.
Upper Rump: black, using burnt umber and black. Curls are black.
Sides: light-medium gray, using black, white, and burnt umber, vermiculated with a brownish gray.
Chest Color: equal amounts of burnt sienna and burnt umber. (chestnut color) Faint feather edges of white, washed with the base color.
Center of Back: burnt umber with touch of white added. Also, same color through the scapulars and into the tertials.
Tertials: lighter toward the center and the inside edges. The outside edges are dark; burnt umber.
Secondaries: ultra-marine blue with a touch of white—outer edges black.
Primaries: burnt umber with white, darker edges, lighter toward the center.
Trailing edge of white; leading edge of white banded with black on the insides of the two white edges.
Head Color: thalo green with touch of yellow-green in the cheek, blended so that there is just a lightness in the cheek area, or a lighter hue of the thalo color. Black, wet blended into the crown and down the back of the neck. White ring around the neck about ¼ of an inch wide, jagged, both into the head and into the chest with a gap about one inch directly in back of the head.
Bill Color: yellow ochre. Add tiny bit of white.
Feet: reddish orange.
Nail and Nostrils: black. Final wash of black.

MALLARD DRAKE

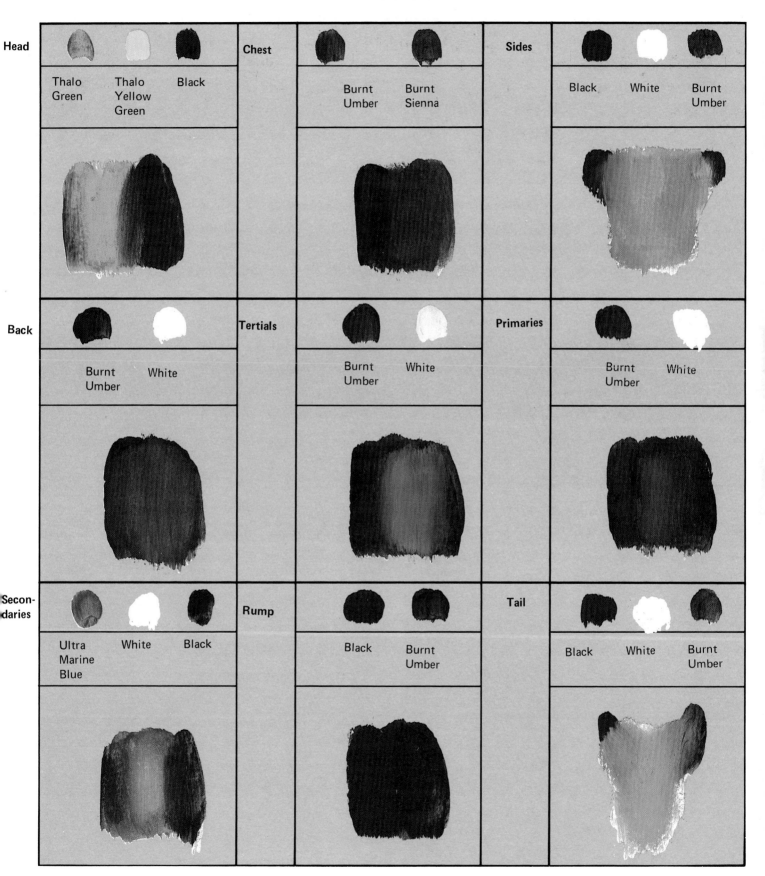

Head

Thalo Green   Thalo Yellow Green   Black

Chest

Burnt Umber   Burnt Sienna

Sides

Black   White   Burnt Umber

Back

Burnt Umber   White

Tertials

Burnt Umber   White

Primaries

Burnt Umber   White

Secondaries

Ultra Marine Blue   White   Black

Rump

Black   Burnt Umber

Tail

Black   White   Burnt Umber

45

Mallard hen decorative decoy by Sina ''Pat'' Kurman

Mallard hen decorative decoy — head and bill detail

Mallard hen decorative decoy — back and tail area

Mallard hen decorative decoy — tertials, primaries and tail

Mallard hen — threatening position

46

Mallard drake — back and side area

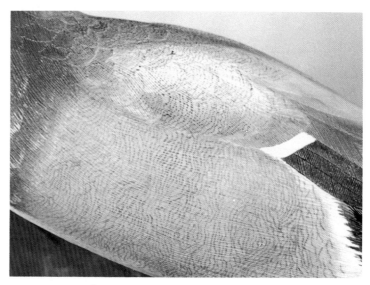

Mallard drake — side detail

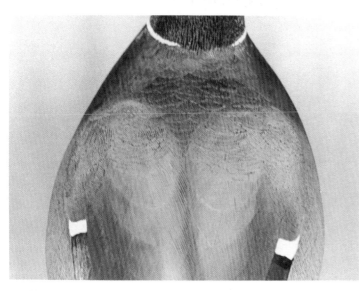

Mallard Drake—back detail

Mallard drake — primaries and tail detail

Mallard drake decorative decoy — secondaries — tertials and tail area

Mallard drake decorative decoy — head and bill detail

Mallard Drake

Mallard drake decorative decoy — head detail

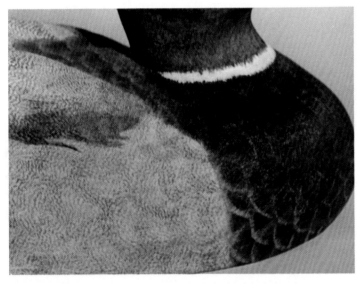
Mallard drake decorative decoy — chest and side area

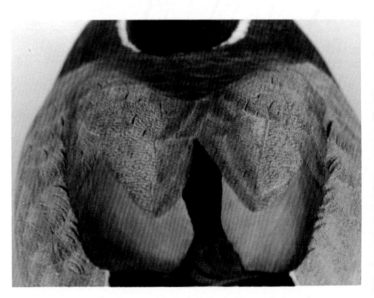
Mallard drake decorative decoy — tertials and primaries

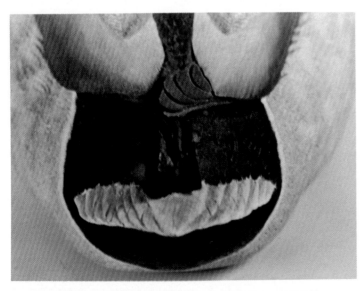
Mallard drake decorative decoy — primaries and tail detail

Mallard drake decorative decoy — side and tail detail

Mallard drake — head, crown and bill

Mallard drake — belly and speculum

Mallard drake — spread wing — speculum detail

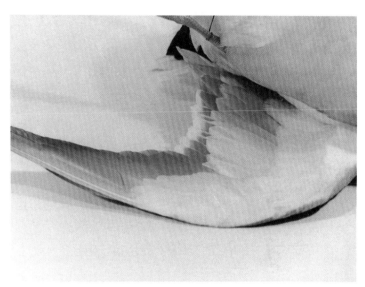

Mallard drake — under wing detail

Mallard drake — primaries — tertials — tail area —
note position of curl

Mallard drake — rump detail

Pair of mallards

Mallard drake standing

Mallard drake swimming

Pintail hen decorative decoy — by Penny Mace

Pintail hen decorative decoy — head — chest — bill — bill detail

Species: Pintail
Sex: Hen

PAINTING INSTRUCTIONS

Color list: *Black, White, Burnt umber, Raw sienna, Payne's Gray.*

Sides: resemble a Mallard Hen, only a much lighter edged. Each feather is edged more deeply with raw sienna and white, with more white.

Back and Wing area: resembles that of a Mallard Wing. Basically dark in color; dark brown in color, edged with a buffy color, using raw sienna, white. Lighter than the Mallard Hen.

Secondaries: irridescence coppery with a trailing edge of white, and leading edge of tan, using raw sienna and white.

Primaries: burnt umber with a touch of white. Outside edges darker, inside lighter in hue.

Head: Raw sienna and white, touch of burnt umber, crown darker using burnt umber. Streaks and eye line; burnt umber with a touch of black.

Bill: bluish gray, using Payne's gray and white. And touch of burnt umber.

Feet: steely gray, using black and white to make the gray.

Pintail hen decorative decoy — head and bill detail

51

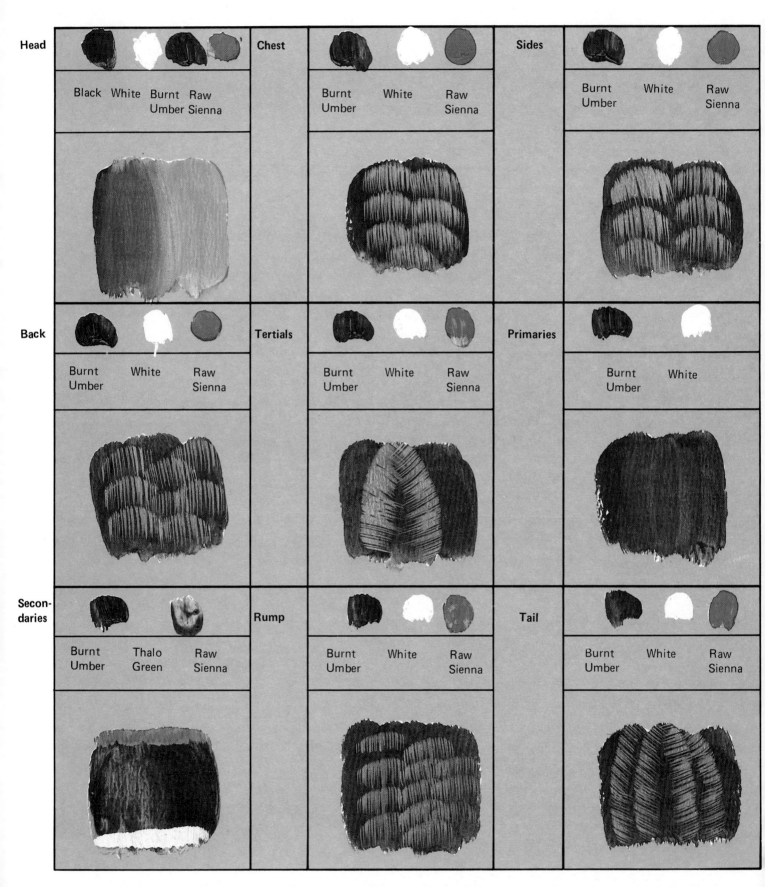

Head

Black White Burnt Umber Raw Sienna

Chest

Burnt Umber   White   Raw Sienna

Sides

Burnt Umber   White   Raw Sienna

Back

Burnt Umber   White   Raw Sienna

Tertials

Burnt Umber   White   Raw Sienna

Primaries

Burnt Umber   White

Secondaries

Burnt Umber   Thalo Green   Raw Sienna

Rump

Burnt Umber   White   Raw Sienna

Tail

Burnt Umber   White   Raw Sienna

Pintail hen decorative decoy — primaries and tail detail

Pintail hen decorative decoy — back detail

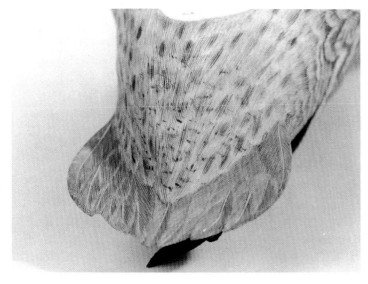

Pintail hen decorative decoy — rump area

Pintail hen decorative decoy — side detail

Pintail hen decorative decoy — primaries and tail detail

Pintail hen decorative — crown and back detail

Exotic hen

Pair Pintails

Pintail Drake

Pintail drake decorative decoy by Hal Hopkins

Pintail drake decorative decoy—tertial area

Pintail drake decorative decoy — head and neck detail

Pintail drake — preening position

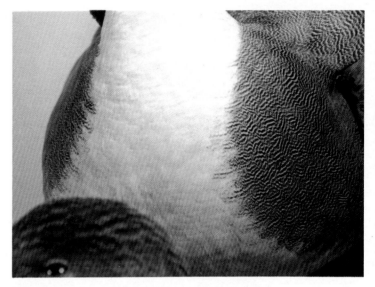

Pintail drake — chest detail — crown detail

Pintail drake — preening position

Pintail drake — rump detail

Pintail Drake

Pintail drake — rump area

Pintail drake — side view

Pintail drake — rear view

Pair Pintails

Pintail drake decorative carving by Ralph Moffet

Pintail drake decorative carving—tail detail

Pintail drake decorative carving—back detail

Species: Pintail
Sex: Drake

PAINTING INSTRUCTIONS

Color list: *Black, White, Burnt umber, Payne's gray, Yellow ochre, Raw sienna, Thalo bronze, ultra-marine blue.*
Base Colors for Pintail Drake:
Tail: medium gray, using black, white, and burnt umber to mix the gray.
Tail Covert: edged with white to a yellowish white, using yellow ochre, mostly white.
Tail Feathers: edged in white. Center feather is black. Vermiculated area is vermiculated with black. The undercoating of white should have some burnt umber in it so that it's not a stark white.
Rump and Under Rump: black.
Foreback and Sides, Belly and Chest: undercoat with white.
Scapulars and Tertial Area: burnt umber with black, mixed with ultra-marine blue.
Scapulars and Tertial Feathers: edged with light gray to white.
Secondaries: irridescenct coppery with a trailing edge of white, and leading edge of tan, using raw sienna and white.
Primaries: burnt umber with a touch of white. Darker on the edges, lighter in the interior.
Head: undercoat with burnt umber. Darker on the crown, lighter in the cheek area. Lighten the burnt umber by adding white. Sometimes there is a rose or purplish irridescence in the back part of the cheek area.
Bill Color: **Base**: black. The bluish-gray patch is made with Payne's gray and white.
Feet: steely gray, using black and white to make the gray.
Webs: blackish.
Toes: have black bars across them.
Nails: black.

PINTAIL DRAKE

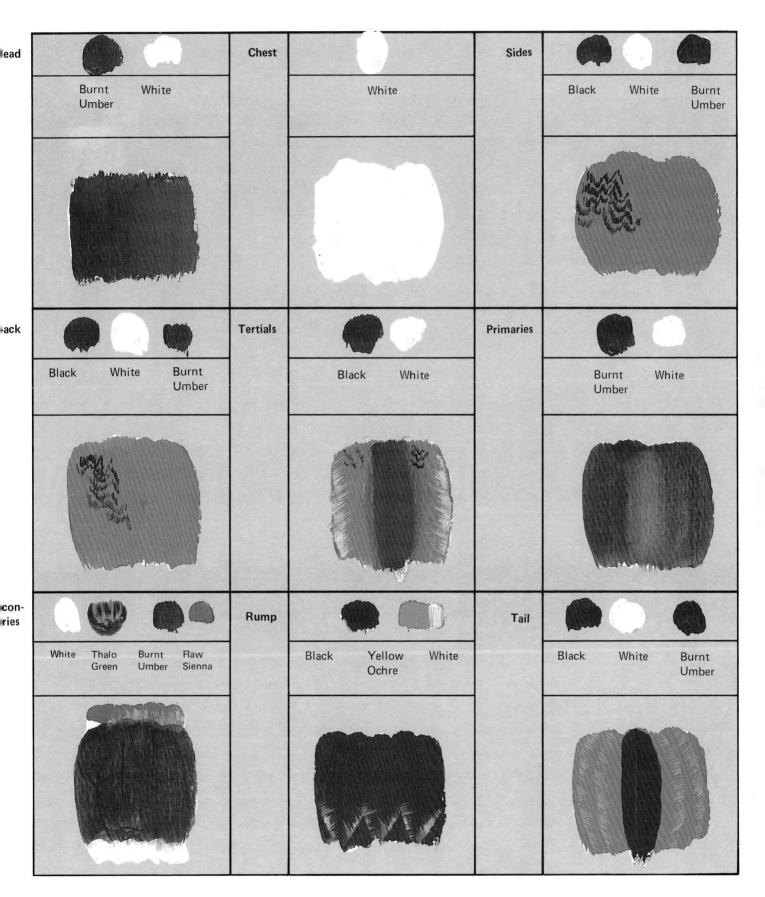

Head
Burnt Umber · White

Chest
White

Sides
Black · White · Burnt Umber

Back
Black · White · Burnt Umber

Tertials
Black · White

Primaries
Burnt Umber · White

Secondaries
White · Thalo Green · Burnt Umber · Raw Sienna

Rump
Black · Yellow Ochre · White

Tail
Black · White · Burnt Umber

Shoveler Hen — preening

Shoveler Hen — tail detail

Shoveler Hen — back and tail detail

Species: Shoveler
Sex: Hen

PAINTING INSTRUCTIONS

Color list: *Black, White, Burnt umber, Raw sienna, Red, Yellow ochre, Thalo green.*

Shoveler Hen is marked and very similar to the Mallard Hen.
Base Color: Body: burnt umber with a touch of white.
All Feathers: edged with raw sienna and white. Lighter toward the sides and chest.
All Streaks and Spots: burnt umber and touch of black.
Wing: similar to Cinnamon and Blue-Winged Teal: bluish, using Payne's gray and white; touch of burnt umber.
Bill: orangish with dark brown spots mottled with dark brown; brown ridge.
Scapulars: blue, using Payne's gray and white; touch of burnt umber.
Secondaries: thalo green, touch of yellow-green.
Trailing Edge: white.
Secondary Coverts: white.
Primaries: burnt umber with a touch of white. Lighter in the center, darker on the edges.
Head Color: Base Color: raw sienna, white, and touch of burnt umber. Dark around the crown with burnt umber and touch of black. Eyeline as well.
Feet: orangish, using yellow ochre and red.

Shoveler Hen — bill detail

SHOVELER HEN

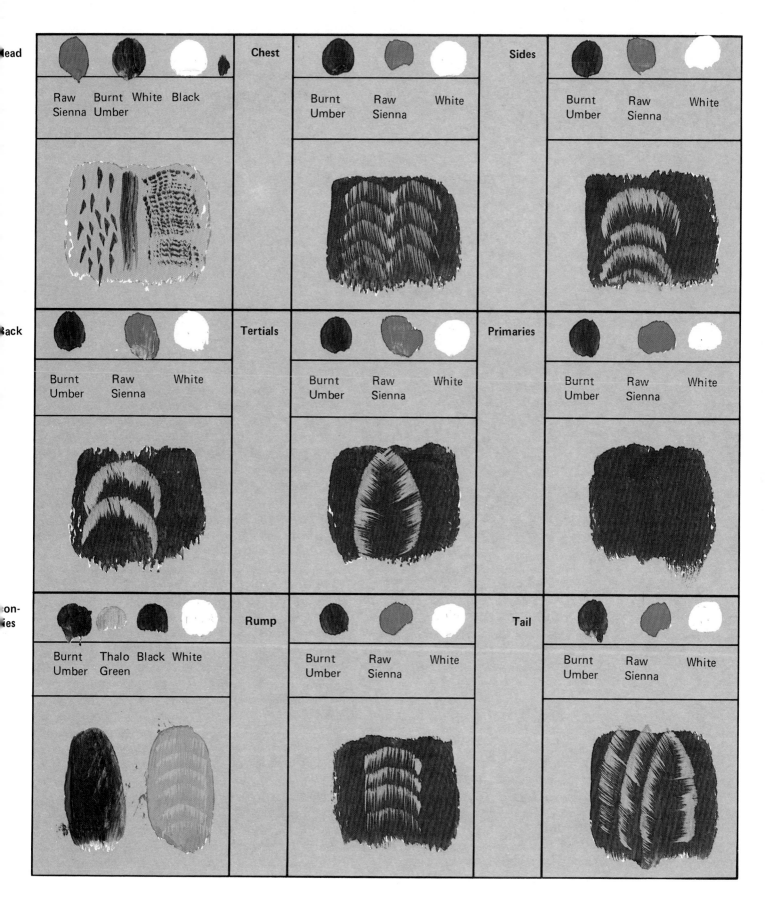

Head
Raw Sienna | Burnt Umber | White | Black

Chest
Burnt Umber | Raw Sienna | White

Sides
Burnt Umber | Raw Sienna | White

Back
Burnt Umber | Raw Sienna | White

Tertials
Burnt Umber | Raw Sienna | White

Primaries
Burnt Umber | Raw Sienna | White

Con-erties
Burnt Umber | Thalo Green | Black | White

Rump
Burnt Umber | Raw Sienna | White

Tail
Burnt Umber | Raw Sienna | White

Shoveler Drake

Shoveler drake — head detail

Shoveler Drake decoy by Martina Martin

Species: Shoveler
Sex: Drake

PAINTING INSTRUCTIONS

Color list: *Black, White, Burnt umber, Raw sienna, Yellow ochre, Burnt sienna, Thalo green, Payne's gray, Thalo yellow-green, Red.*

Tail of Shoveler: undercoat: dusky gray, edged with white.

Under Tail: grayish.

Under Rump and Rump: black with greenish highlights.

Chest: white.

Center of the Back: dark gray edged in white. Along the edge of that area would be part wing. Bluish, same as the hen.

Secondaries: thalo green, touch of yellow-green.

Trailing Edge: white.

Scapulars: bluish, using Payne's gray and white.

Scapulars and Tertials: white. A white edging on a black, white, and burnt umber dark gray area.

Secondary Coverts: white.

Primaries: burnt umber with a touch of white. Darker on the outside; lighter on the inside edges.

Head: thalo green, touch of yellow-green, blended with black through the crown, down the neck.

Bill: black.

Feet. orangish, using yellow ochre and red.

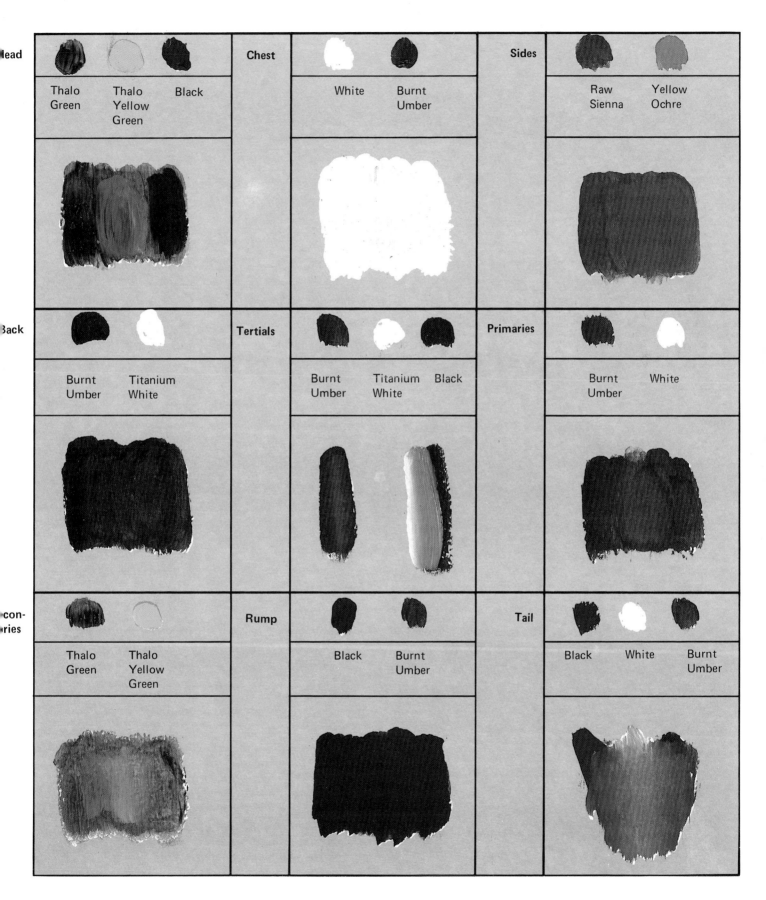

Head			Chest			Sides	
Thalo Green	Thalo Yellow Green	Black		White	Burnt Umber	Raw Sienna	Yellow Ochre

Back		Tertials				Primaries	
Burnt Umber	Titanium White		Burnt Umber	Titanium White	Black	Burnt Umber	White

Secon-daries		Rump			Tail		
Thalo Green	Thalo Yellow Green		Black	Burnt Umber	Black	White	Burnt Umber

Blue Winged teal hen decorative decoy by Penny Mace

Blue Winged teal hen—head and bill detail

Blue Winged teal hen — secondaries and coverts

Species: Blue-Winged Teal
Sex: Hen

PAINTING INSTRUCTIONS

Color list: *Burnt umber, White, Raw sienna, Thalo green, Thalo yellow-green, Black, Payne's gray, Yellow ochre.*
Feathers: burnt umber with a touch of white. Darker on the outside edges; lighter in the interior of the feather.
Body Colors for the Blue-Winged Teal and the Cinnamon Teal Hen:
Tail: burnt umber edged with white. Underside: grayish .
Rump: burnt umber.
Sides and Back: burnt umber with a touch of white. Edged and interior edgings: raw sienna and white.
Inside and Outside: blackish.
Belly: whitish.
Secondary: thalo green with a touch of yellow-green. Trim and edged with white.
Secondary Coverts: paynes gray and white mixed to bluish gray.
Head Color: white with raw sienna, touch of burnt umber for buffy color. A light gray at the head, blended into black at the base. A few black spots under the nostril area.
Eyeline, Crown, and Streaks and Head: burnt umber with a touch of black.
Major portion of the arm of the wing: bluish, using Payne's gray and white; touch of burnt umber.
Bill: gray into black. It's tipped with an orangish edge along the lower edge of the upper mandible.
Feet: yellowish, using yellow ochre.
Webs: gray.
Toes: blackish spots.

BLUE-WINGED TEAL HEN

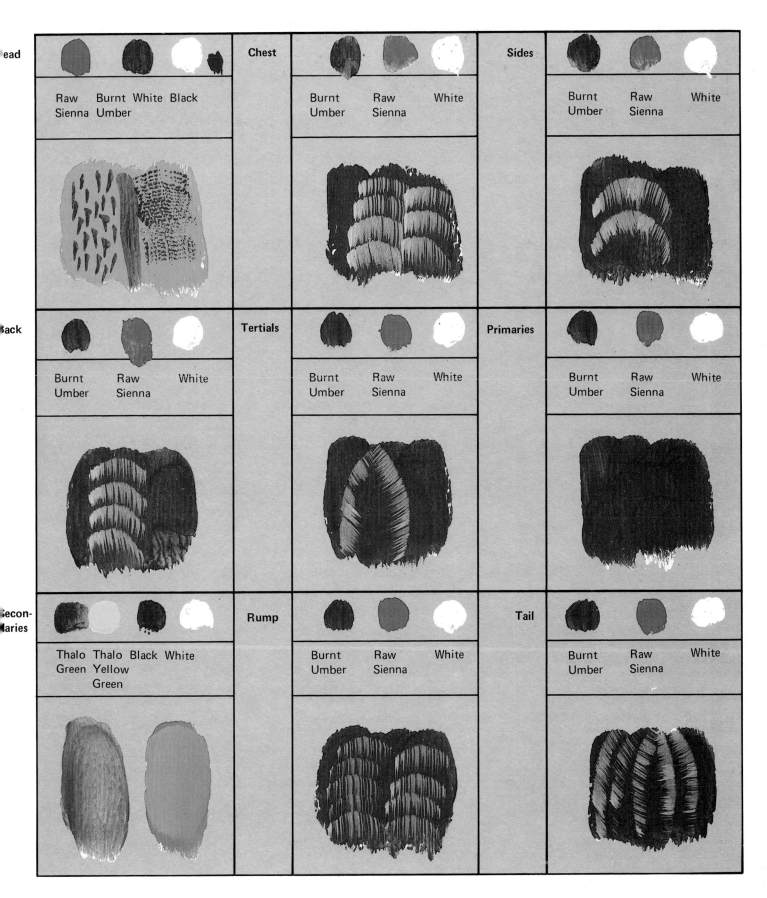

Head

Raw Sienna | Burnt Umber | White | Black

Chest

Burnt Umber | Raw Sienna | White

Sides

Burnt Umber | Raw Sienna | White

Back

Burnt Umber | Raw Sienna | White

Tertials

Burnt Umber | Raw Sienna | White

Primaries

Burnt Umber | Raw Sienna | White

Secondaries

Thalo Green | Thalo Yellow Green | Black | White

Rump

Burnt Umber | Raw Sienna | White

Tail

Burnt Umber | Raw Sienna | White

65

Blue winged teal hen — head detail

Blue winged teal hen — chest detail

Blue winged teal hen — upper wing and belly detail

Blue Winged teal hen — under tail and belly detail

Blue winged teal pair

Blue winged teal drake decorative decoy by Sina "Pat" Kurman

Species: Blue-Winged Teal
Sex: Drake

PAINTING INSTRUCTIONS

Color list: *Black, White, Burnt umber, Raw sienna, Payne's gray, Thalo green, Thalo yellow-green, Yellow ochre.*

There is a light patch just in front of the tail, which is triangular in shape.

The underside of the Tail: dark, silvery gray.

Upper side of the Tail: burnt umber, edged with raw sienna and white.

All Feathers: edged with raw sienna and white.

The spots in the interior of the feathers: burnt umber with a touch of black.

Outside edges: burnt umber. Black under rump, through vent area, up to the tail.

Sides, Belly, and Chest: Base Color: raw sienna and white.

Back of the Blue-Winged Teal: same as the back of Cinnamon Teal: burnt umber with a touch of white. Edged and interior edgings: raw sienna and white. Washed with burnt umber, gradually darkened.

Scapulars: Payne's gray and white, making them blue.

Interior of the Scapular and Tertials: raw sienna and white.

The Wing: Secondaries: thalo green with a touch of yellow green.

Trailing Edge: faint edge with white.

Secondary Coverts: paynes gray mixed with white to make bluish gray.

Primary Colors: burnt umber, touch of white. Dark on the edges: light in the interior.

Head: soft gray, using black, white, and burnt umber to make gray crown blended into black. Also, back of the neck, the white crescent is banded with black.

Bill: black.

Feet: yellowish.

Webs: blackish.

Toes: have black spots.

Nails: black.

BLUE-WINGED TEAL DRAKE

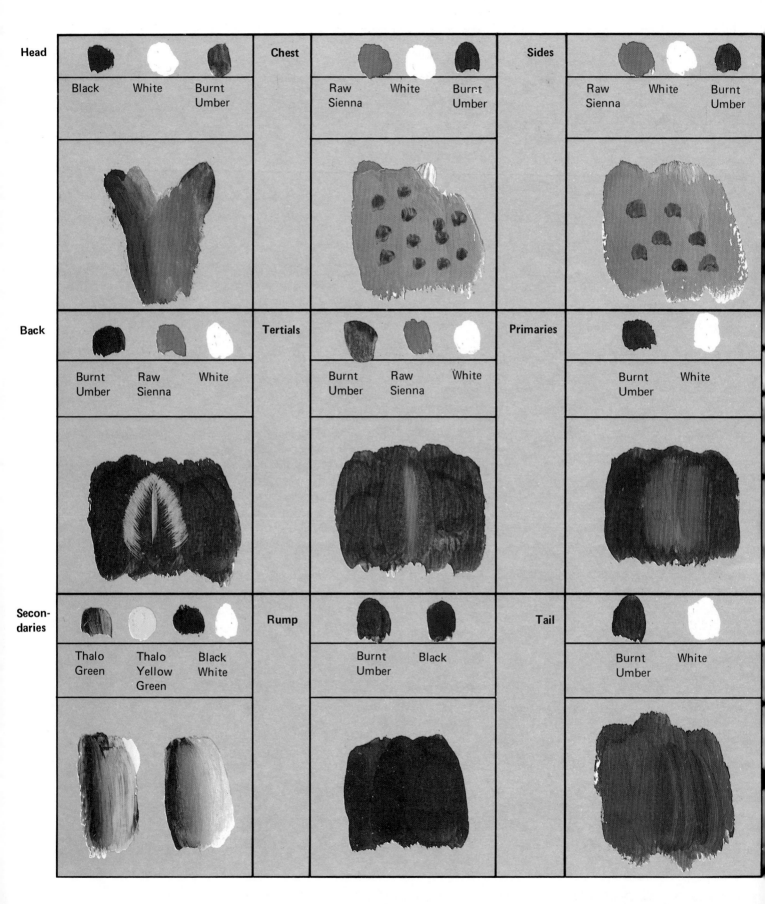

Head

Black White Burnt Umber

Chest

Raw Sienna White Burnt Umber

Sides

Raw Sienna White Burnt Umber

Back

Burnt Umber Raw Sienna White

Tertials

Burnt Umber Raw Sienna White

Primaries

Burnt Umber White

Secondaries

Thalo Green Thalo Yellow Green Black White

Rump

Burnt Umber Black

Tail

Burnt Umber White

Blue winged teal drake — head detail

Blue winged teal drake — belly detail

Blue winged teal drake — wing detail

Blue winged teal drake — tail detail

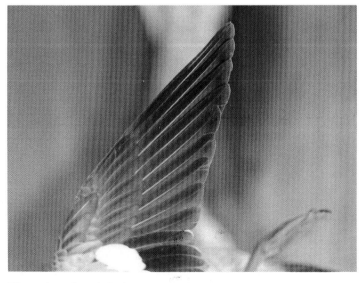

Blue winged teal drake — primary and primary covert

Blue winged teal drake — head detail

Blue winged teal drake decoy — head detail

Blue winged teal drake decoy — head and bill detail

Blue winged teal drake — side detail

Blue winged teal drake — tertials — primary — tail detail

Blue winged teal drake decoy by Sina "Pat" Kurman

Blue winged teal drake decoy — crown detail

70

Cinnamon teal — pair

Cinnamon teal pair—note body position of hen

Species: Cinnamon Teal
Sex: Hen

PAINTING INSTRUCTIONS

Color list: *Burnt umber, White, Raw sienna, Thalo green, Thalo yellow-green, Black, Payne's gray, Yellow ochre.*
Feathers: burnt umber with a touch of white. Darker on the outside edges; lighter in the interior of the feather.
Body Colors for the Cinnamon Teal Hen.
Tail: burnt umber edged with white. Undersie: grayish.
Rump: burnt umber.
Sides and Back: burnt umber with a touch of white. Edged and interior edgings: raw sienna and white.
Inside and Outside: blackish.
Belly: whitish.
Secondary: thalo green with a touch of yellow-green. Trim and edged with white.
Secondary Coverts: white.
Head Color: white with raw sienna, touch of burnt umber for buffy color. A light gray at the head, blended into black at the base. A few black spots under the nostril area.
Eyeline, Crown, and Streaks and Head: burnt umber with a touch of black.
Major portion of the arm of the wing: bluish, using Payne's gray and white; touch of burnt umber.
Bill: gray into black. It's tipped with an orangish edge along the lower edge of the upper mandible.
Feet: yellowish, using yellow ochre.
Webs: gray.
Toes: blackish spots.

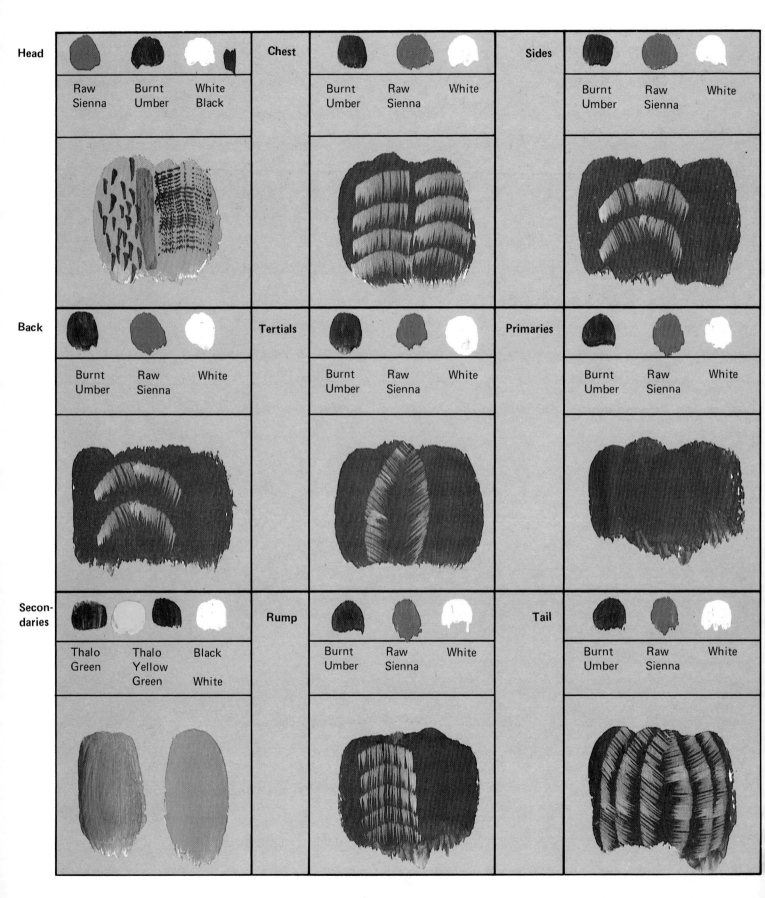

Head

Raw Sienna · Burnt Umber · White Black

Chest

Burnt Umber · Raw Sienna · White

Sides

Burnt Umber · Raw Sienna · White

Back

Burnt Umber · Raw Sienna · White

Tertials

Burnt Umber · Raw Sienna · White

Primaries

Burnt Umber · Raw Sienna · White

Secondaries

Thalo Green · Thalo Yellow Green · Black White

Rump

Burnt Umber · Raw Sienna · White

Tail

Burnt Umber · Raw Sienna · White

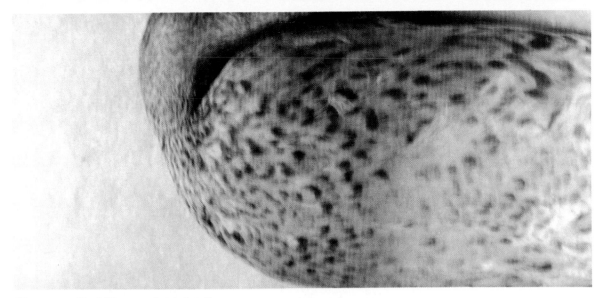

Cinnamon Teal Hen — chest detail

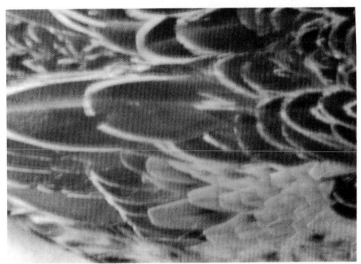

Cinnamon teal hen — secondaries and secondaries coverts

Cinnamon teal hen — secondaries and tail detail

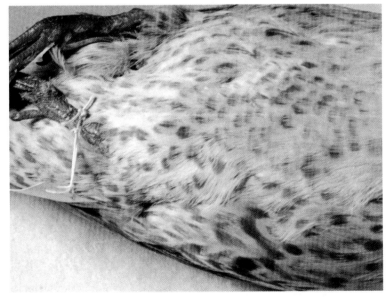

Cinnamon teal hen — belly detail

Cinnamon teal drakes—swimming

Cinnamon teal drake—back, tertials, primaries

Species: Cinnamon Teal
Sex: Drake

PAINTING INSTRUCTIONS

Color list: *Black, White, Burnt umber, Burnt sienna, Yellow ochre, Thalo green, Thalo yellow-green, Raw sienna, cadmium red.*

Tail and Rump: burnt umber, blended into black on the under rump.

Tail Coverts: edged with raw sienna and white.

All Feathers: edged with raw sienna and white.

Feather Edges: a lighter hue of burnt sienna with yellow ochre.

Sides, Chest: burnt sienna with yellow ochre.

The Back of the Cinnamon Teal: burnt umber with a touch of white. Edged and interior edgings: raw sienna and white.

Base Colors: burnt umber with a touch of white, gradually darkening to its full burnt umber.

Scapulars and Tertial Feathers: interiors are much lighter, using raw sienna and white, wet blended with burnt umber edges. Arm of the wing in front of the secondaries is blue, using Payne's gray and white, with a touch of burnt umber.

Secondaries: thalo green with a touch of yellow-green.

Trailing edge: white.

Secondary Coverts: white.

Primaries: burnt umber, touch of white.

Head: burnt sienna with a touch of cadmium red.

Crown: blended with burnt umber.

Bill: black.

Feet: yellowish.

Webs: blackish.

Toes: spotted with black.

CINNAMON TEAL DRAKE

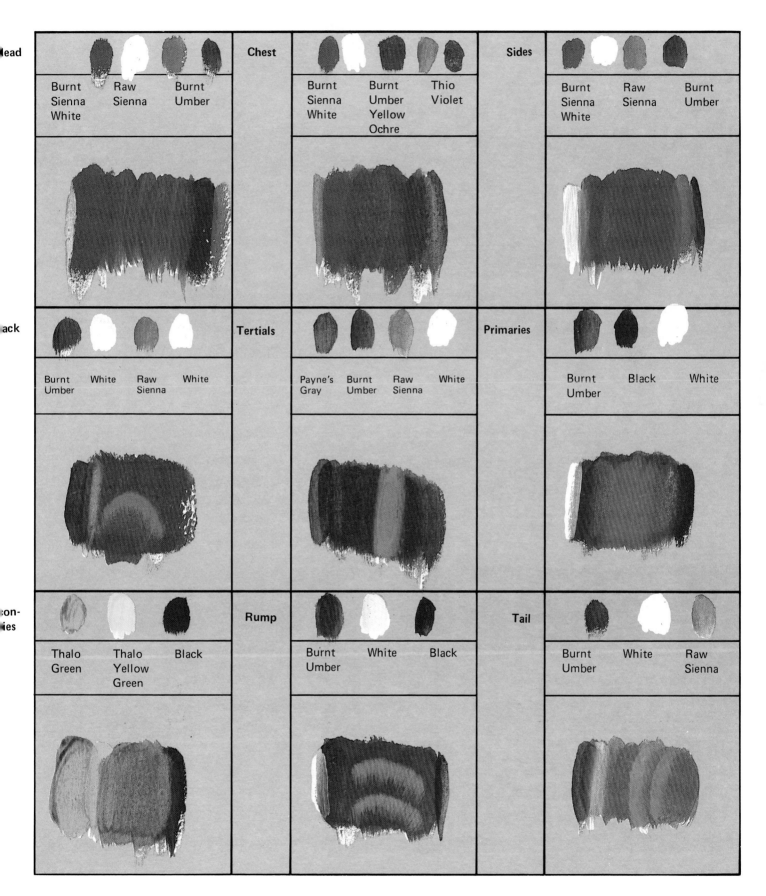

Head		
Burnt Sienna White	Raw Sienna	Burnt Umber

Chest		
Burnt Sienna White	Burnt Umber Yellow Ochre	Thio Violet

Sides		
Burnt Sienna White	Raw Sienna	Burnt Umber

Back			
Burnt Umber	White	Raw Sienna	White

Tertials			
Payne's Gray	Burnt Umber	Raw Sienna	White

Primaries		
Burnt Umber	Black	White

Secon-daries		
Thalo Green	Thalo Yellow Green	Black

Rump		
Burnt Umber	White	Black

Tail		
Burnt Umber	White	Raw Sienna

Cinnamon teal drake — head detail

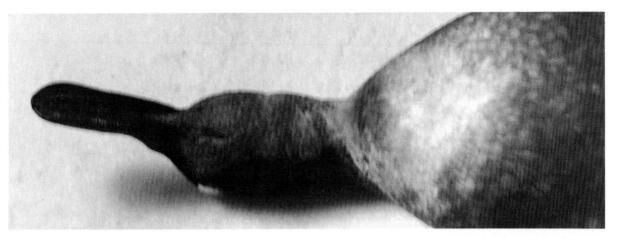

Cinnamon teal drake — chest detail

Cinnamon teal drake — belly detail

Cinnamon teal drake — side and wing detail

Green winged teal hen decorative decoy by Sina "Pat" Kurman

Green winged teal hen decorative decoy — crown and back detail

Green winged teal hen decorative decoy — front detail

Species: Green-Winged Teal
Sex: Hen

PAINTING INSTRUCTIONS

Color list: *Burnt umber, White, Raw sienna, Black, Thalo green, Thalo yellow-green.*
All Feathers: edged with raw sienna and white.
Tail: burnt umber edged with white. Underside: grayish.
Color: burnt umber with a touch of white.
Rump: burnt umber.
Sides and Back: burnt umber with a touch of white. Edged and interior edgings: raw sienna and white.
Inside and Outside: blackish.
Belly: whitish.
Secondary: Same as Drake: thalo green with a touch of yellow-green.
Secondary Coverts: raw sienna with a touch of white.
Secondaries: trim and edged with white.
Head Color: white with raw sienna, touch of burnt umber for buffy color. A light gray at the head, blended into black at the base. A few black spots under the nostril area.
Eyeline, Crown, and Streaks and Head: burnt umber with a touch of black.
Bill: a black and white mixture to make gray.
Feet: medium gray.
Webs: blackish.
Toes: spots of black.
Nail: black.

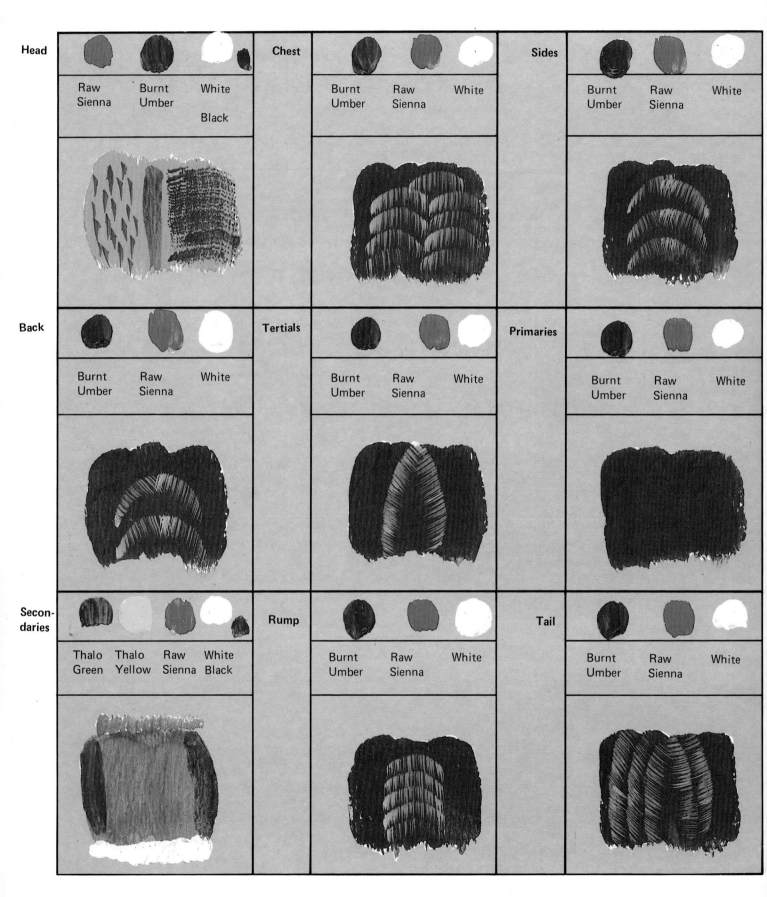

Head
Raw Sienna | Burnt Umber | White | Black

Chest
Burnt Umber | Raw Sienna | White

Sides
Burnt Umber | Raw Sienna | White

Back
Burnt Umber | Raw Sienna | White

Tertials
Burnt Umber | Raw Sienna | White

Primaries
Burnt Umber | Raw Sienna | White

Secondaries
Thalo Green | Thalo Yellow | Raw Sienna | White | Black

Rump
Burnt Umber | Raw Sienna | White

Tail
Burnt Umber | Raw Sienna | White

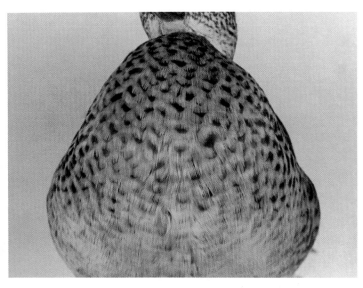

Green winged teal hen — chest detail

Green winged teal hen — primaries and tail detail

Green winged teal hen — chest, side and secondaries

Green winged teal hen decorative decoy — primaries and tail detail

Green winged teal hen decorative decoy — side — secondaries — primaries — tail

Green winged teal hen decorative decoy — wing detail

Green winged teal hen decorative decoy — streaking head

Green winged teal hen decorative decoy — wing edging — arm of wing

Green winged teal hen decorative decoy — head, blending, bill

Green winged teal hen decorative decoy — head, painting bill

Green winged teal hen decorative decoy — edging primaries

Green winged teal hen decorative decoy — final edging on tailing edge of secondaries

80

Green winged teal drake decorative decoy by Sina "Pat" Kurman

Green winged teal drake decorative decoy — front view head — bill and chest detail

Species: Green-Winged Teal
Sex: Drake

PAINTING INSTRUCTIONS

Color list: *Black, White, Burnt umber, Burnt sienna, Yellow ochre, Thalo green, Thalo yellow-green, Raw sienna.*
Tail: dusky gray, edged with white.
Under Rump: yellow ochre patch on either side, split in the center with black, edged with black torbid ball.
Upper Rump: black, edged with pale yellow and tail coverts.
Sides and Back: undercoat with light gray. Vermiculated with black and with white.
Chest: white, raw sienna, touch of burnt sienna.
Belly: whitish.
Scapulars and Tertials: grayish, edged with raw sienna, white.
Secondaries: thalo green with touch of yellow-green; inside and outside. Feathers washed with black.
Secondary Coverts: raw sienna with a touch of white.
Trailing edge of Secondaries: white.
Primaries: burnt umber with a touch of white. Light in the center; dark on the edges.
Head: burnt sienna. Yellow ochre blended in the cheek. Black blended at the base of the crest and under the chin. Burnt umber blended along the crown line.
Eye Patch: thalo green with touch of yellow-green, edged with a thin line of yellow ochre, white, and burnt sienna.
Bill: black.
Feet: steely gray—light gray.
Webs: blackish
Toe Nails: black.

Green winged teal drake decorative decoy — head and bill detail

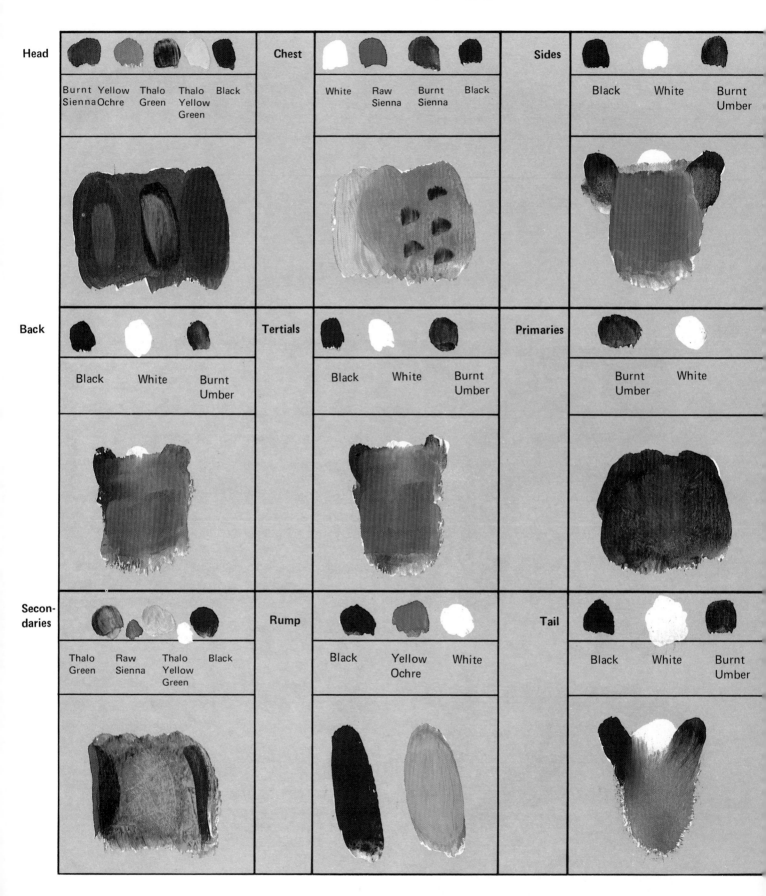

Head
Burnt Sienna · Yellow Ochre · Thalo Green · Thalo Yellow Green · Black

Chest
White · Raw Sienna · Burnt Sienna · Black

Sides
Black · White · Burnt Umber

Back
Black · White · Burnt Umber

Tertials
Black · White · Burnt Umber

Primaries
Burnt Umber · White

Secondaries
Thalo Green · Raw Sienna · Thalo Yellow Green · Black

Rump
Black · Yellow Ochre · White

Tail
Black · White · Burnt Umber

Green winged teal drake decorative decoy — side — tail primaries and tertials

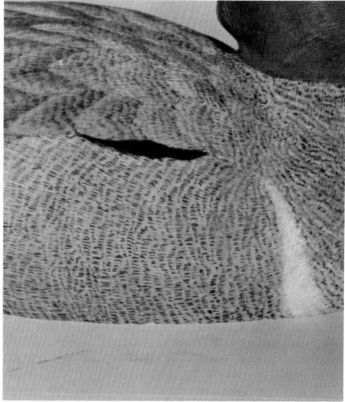

Green winged teal drake decorative decoy — side detail

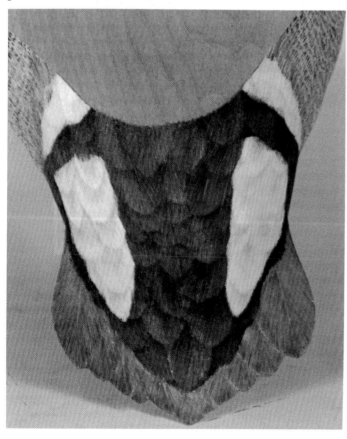

Green winged teal drake decorative decoy — rump area

Green winged teal drake decorative decoy — tertials, primaries and tail detail

Green winged teal drake — side detail

Green winged teal drake — tertials detail — note position of tertials and green patch

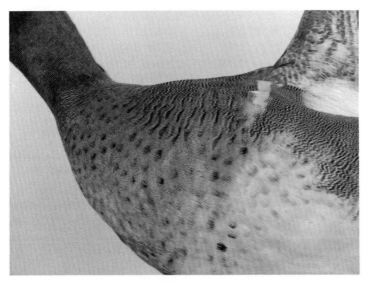
Green winged teal drake — side and chest area

Green winged teal drake — head and bill detail

Green winged teal drake — detail of spread wings

Green winged teal drake — swimming

Green winged teal drake — rump detail

Green winged teal drake — chest area

Green winged teal drake — back view with wings spread

Green winged teal drake — underside of spread wings

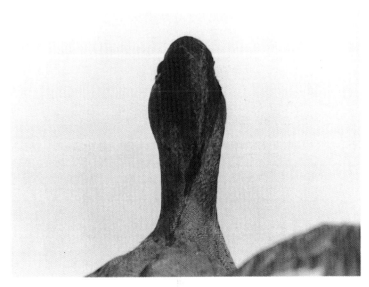
Green winged teal drake — crown detail

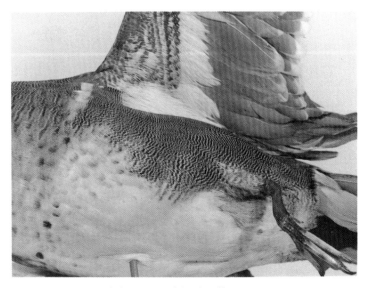
Green winged teal drake — side detail

Green winged teal pair—decoratives by Ralph Moffett

Green winged teal pair—decoratives by Ralph Moffett

American Widgeon Drake — side and neck detail

American Widgeon Drake — chest belly and side area

American Widgeon Drake — chest and belly detail

American Widgeon drake — primaries and tail detail

Species: American Widgeon
Sex: Drake

PAINTING INSTRUCTIONS

Color list: *Black, White, Burnt umber, Alizeron crimson, Thalo violet, Panye's gray, Thalo green, Thalo yellow-green.*
Back and Sides: undercoat with thalo violet or Alizeron crimson, a little white and burnt umber.
All Back Feathers and Side Feathers: vermiculated with black.
Chest: a lighter hue of the side color. Just add white.
Tertial Feathers: a black and gray combination, edged with white. Half of each.
Primaries: burnt umber with a touch of white.
Head: undercoat of white with a touch of burnt umber.
Eye Patch: black and green, using thalo green with a touch of yellow-green.
Crown: white.
Bill: Payne's gray and white, bluish gray.
Nail: black.

American widgeon drake decorative decoy by Jack Alderson

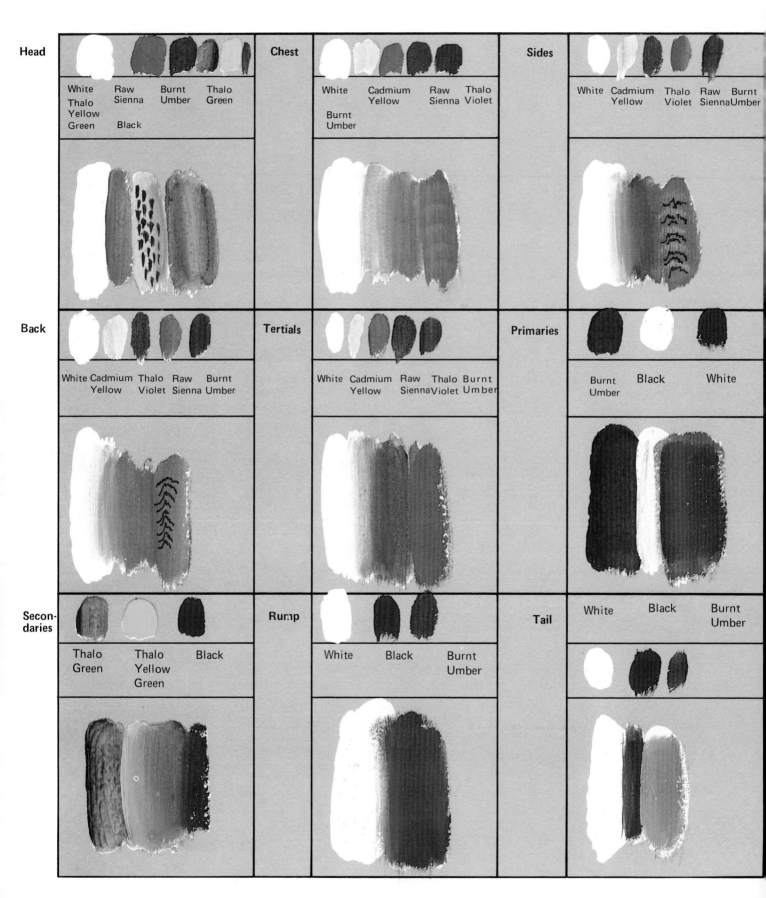

Head

White
Thalo
Yellow
Green   Raw   Burnt   Thalo
         Sienna Umber   Green
         Black

Chest

White   Cadmium   Raw   Thalo
         Yellow   Sienna Violet
Burnt
Umber

Sides

White Cadmium   Thalo   Raw   Burnt
       Yellow   Violet Sienna Umber

Back

White Cadmium Thalo   Raw   Burnt
       Yellow   Violet Sienna Umber

Tertials

White Cadmium Raw   Thalo   Burnt
       Yellow   Sienna Violet Umber

Primaries

Burnt   Black   White
Umber

Secondaries

Thalo   Thalo   Black
Green   Yellow
             Green

Rump

White   Black   Burnt
                          Umber

Tail

White   Black   Burnt
                          Umber

Wood Duck Hen

Wood Duck hen — head detail

Wood duck hen — chest detail

Species: Wood Duck
Sex: Hen

PAINTING INSTRUCTIONS

Color list: *Black, White, Burnt umber, Raw sienna, Raw umber, Ultra-marine blue, Thalo violet, iridescent white.*
Tail: burnt umber, touch of white.
Tail Feathers: edged in black.
Rump: burnt umber, touch of white.
Sides: raw umber, touch of white.
Chest: raw umber, touch of white.
Side and Chest Feathers: interior and faint edging with raw sienna, mixed with white.
Belly: whitish.
Back: burnt umber, touch of white.
Back Feathers and Wing Feathers: edged in black.
Secondaries: ultra-marine blue.
Secondary coverts: thalo violet.
Primary Feathers: inside arc: bluish. Outside: base with burnt umber, edged with white. Second edging of iridescent white. Use iridescence sparingly throughout the back and primary feathers—tail feathers and head.
Head: soft dusky gray, mix black, white, and burnt umber. Whitish under chin and around eye. A bit greenish and blackish through the crown and crest.
Bill: medium gray, lighter around nostril.
Feet: yellow ochre, bands of black.
Webs: blackish.
Nails: black.

WOOD DUCK HEN

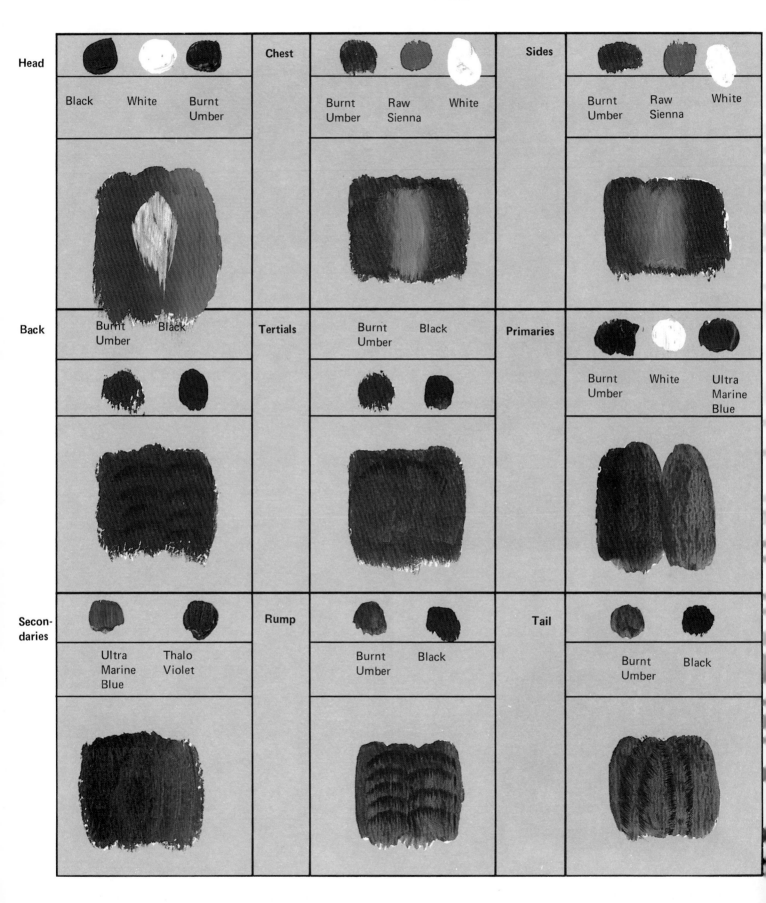

Head — Black · White · Burnt Umber

Chest — Burnt Umber · Raw Sienna · White

Sides — Burnt Umber · Raw Sienna · White

Back — Burnt Umber · Black

Tertials — Burnt Umber · Black

Primaries — Burnt Umber · White · Ultra Marine Blue

Secondaries — Ultra Marine Blue · Thalo Violet

Rump — Burnt Umber · Black

Tail — Burnt Umber · Black

Wood duck hen — side detail

Wood duck hen — chest and belly

Wood duck hen—tertial detail

Wood duck hen — tail and primary detail

Wood duck hen — under tail detail

Wood duck hen — secondaries and secondaries coverts

Wood duck drake

Decorative wood duck drake decoy by Jack Alderson

Species: Wood Duck
Sex: Drake

PAINTING INSTRUCTIONS

Color list: *Black, White, Burnt umber, Thalo violet, Thalo green, Thalo yellow-green, Napthol crimson or Alizaron crimson, Ultra-marine blue, Burnt sienna, Yellow ochre.*
Iridescence: *White, Green, Rose, Blue.*
Tail: black with ultra-marine blue and patches of thalo green—wet blended.
Under Tail: black with ultra-marine blue and patches of thalo green.
Rump: black with ultra-marine blue and patches of thalo green. Separation between sides and chest, breast and chest, will be a black bar and a white bar. White in front.
Chest: burnt umber, burnt sienna, and thalo violet.
Chest Pyramids: white. In the rump area there is a salmon colored stripe, red, white, and raw sienna to make the salmon color.
Back: black with ultra-marine blue and patches of thalo green.
Tertials: bluish and greenish.
Secondaries: ultra-marine blue. Trailing edge of secondaries: white. Sides: yellow ochre with touch of white and vermiculate sides with black. Side pocket white stripes banded with black front and back.
Secondary coverts: thalo violet.
Primary Feathers: inside arc: bluish. Outside: base with burnt umber, edged with white. Second edging of iridescent white. Use iridescence sparingly throughout the back and primary feathers—tail feathers and head.
Head: white, patch of white, touch of burnt umber.
Balance of Head: thalo green, touch of violet, crown and crest blended with black, touch of yellow-green, blended in cheek.
Eye lid: red.
Bill: red, white, and black, banded with yellow ochre next to head.
Feet: yellow ochre with black bars.
Webs: blackish.

WOOD DUCK DRAKE

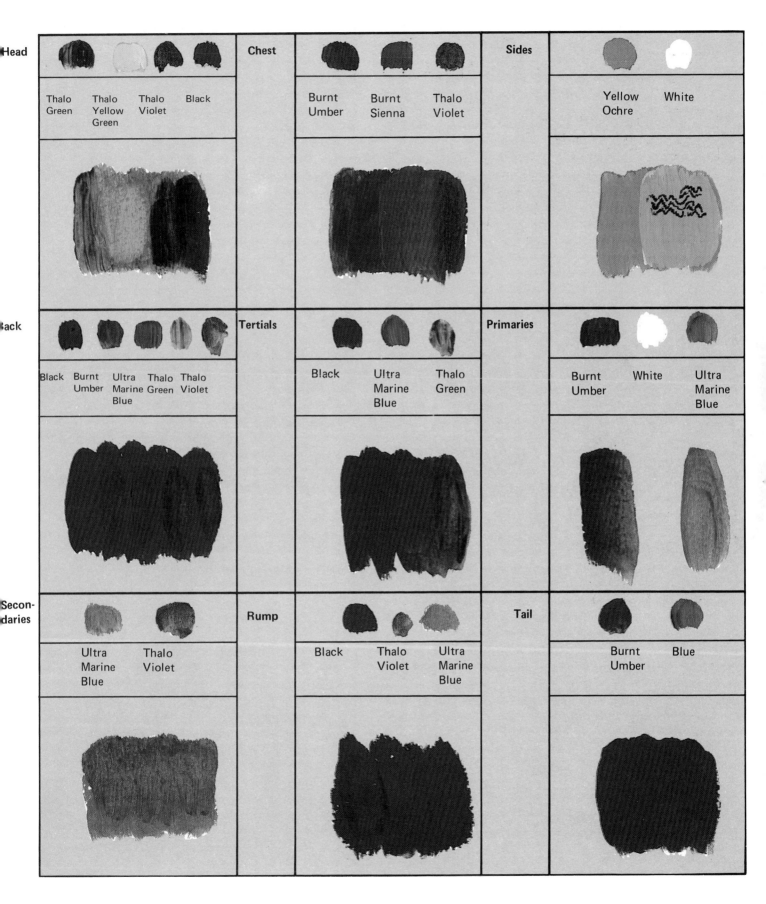

Head

Thalo Green | Thalo Yellow Green | Thalo Violet | Black

Chest

Burnt Umber | Burnt Sienna | Thalo Violet

Sides

Yellow Ochre | White

Back

Black | Burnt Umber | Ultra Marine Blue | Thalo Green | Thalo Violet

Tertials

Black | Ultra Marine Blue | Thalo Green

Primaries

Burnt Umber | White | Ultra Marine Blue

Secondaries

Ultra Marine Blue | Thalo Violet

Rump

Black | Thalo Violet | Ultra Marine Blue

Tail

Burnt Umber | Blue

Wood duck drake — head detail

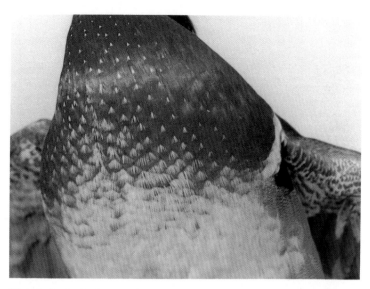

Wood duck drake — chest area

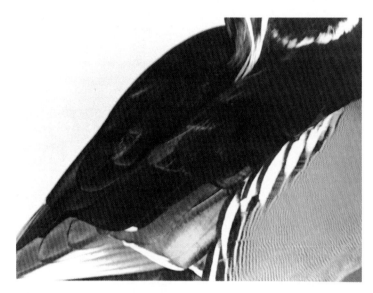

Wood duck drake — tertials primaries and secondaries

Wood duck drake — wing detail

Wood duck drake — tail and primaries detail

Wood duck drake — head, crown and back detail

Wood duck drake carving — detail

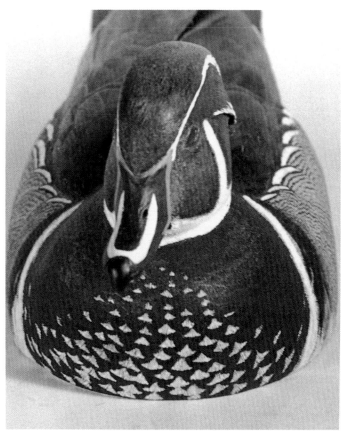

Wood duck drake carving — chest detail

Wood duck drake — primaries

Bufflehead drake — profile

Bufflehead drake — crest and crown detail

Bufflehead drake — head — crest and bill detail

Species: Buffle Head
Sex: Drake

PAINTING INSTRUCTIONS

Color list: *Black, White, Burnt umber, Thalo violet, Thalo green, Payne's gray, Napthol crimson or Cadmium red, Raw sienna.*
Tail: dusky gray, using black, white, and burnt umber.
Tail Coverts: whitish.
Rump and under Rump: dusky gray with black, white, and burnt umber; darkening as it goes forward in the body.
Sides, Chest, and Belly: white.
Back: black mixed with burnt umber.
Neck: white.
Head: white patch on the head. The head is thalo green with a touch of violet in the cheek. Black in the crown.
Bill: Payne's gray and white with a touch of burnt umber.
Feet: pinkish, made with red and white, using a touch of raw sienna.
Nail: black.

BUFFLEHEAD DRAKE

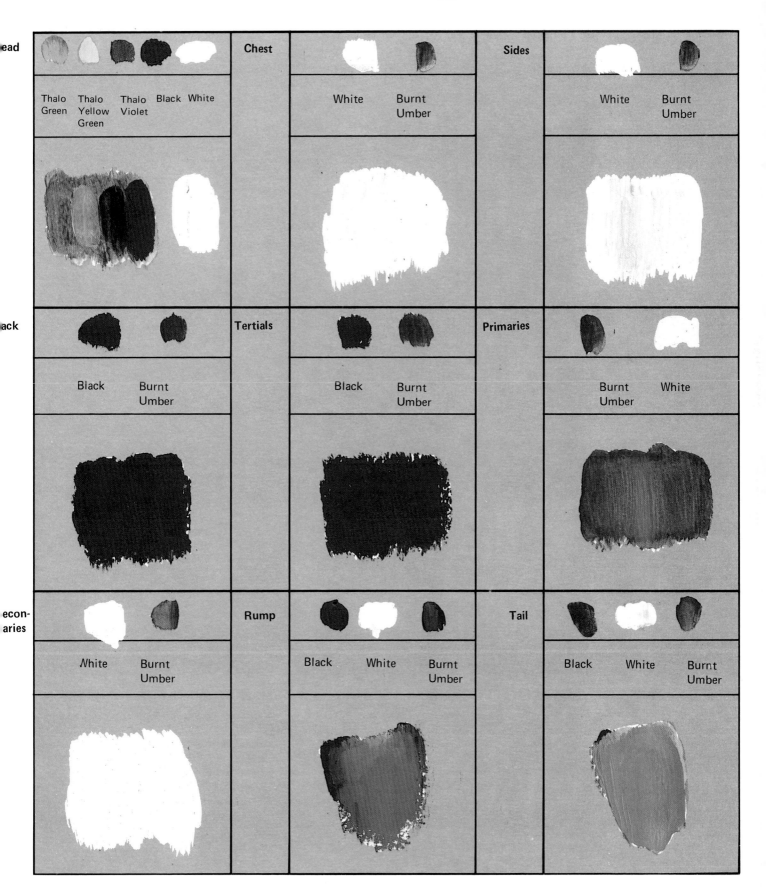

Head

Thalo Green | Thalo Yellow Green | Thalo Violet | Black | White

Chest

White | Burnt Umber

Sides

White | Burnt Umber

Back

Black | Burnt Umber

Tertials

Black | Burnt Umber

Primaries

Burnt Umber | White

Secondaries

White | Burnt Umber

Rump

Black | White | Burnt Umber

Tail

Black | White | Burnt Umber

Bufflehead drake — primaries and tail area detail

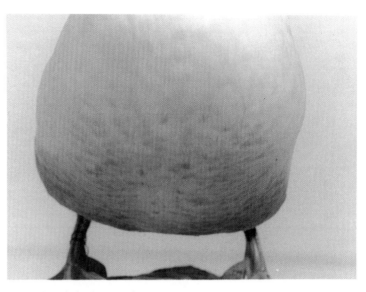

Bufflehead drake — chest and belly area

Bufflehead drake — side view — note black and white detail

Bufflehead drake — back, sides into tail detail

Bufflehead drake swimming

Bufflehead drake swimming

Bufflehead hen decoy by Jack Alderson

Bufflehead hen decoy — head, cheek and bill detail

Bufflehead hen swimming

Species: Buffle Head
Sex: Hen

PAINTING INSTRUCTIONS

Color list: *Black, White, Burnt umber, Ultra-marine blue, Red, Raw sienna.*
Ultra-marine blue and burnt umber to make blackish-brown. Paint the back, upper part of the sides. Paint the lower third of the body white, using a dry, soft brush. Blend the two colors. Go from white upward to back with black in the general blend.
Side Feathers: edged with white. Wash with burnt umber. Chest is lighter.
Secondaries: white, as are the secondaries of the drake.
Primaries: burnt umber, touch of white; a little darker than the drake.
Head color: burnt umber; white patch.
Bill: the bill is gray, using Payne's gray, white, and burnt umber.
Feet: flesh color.
Nail: black.

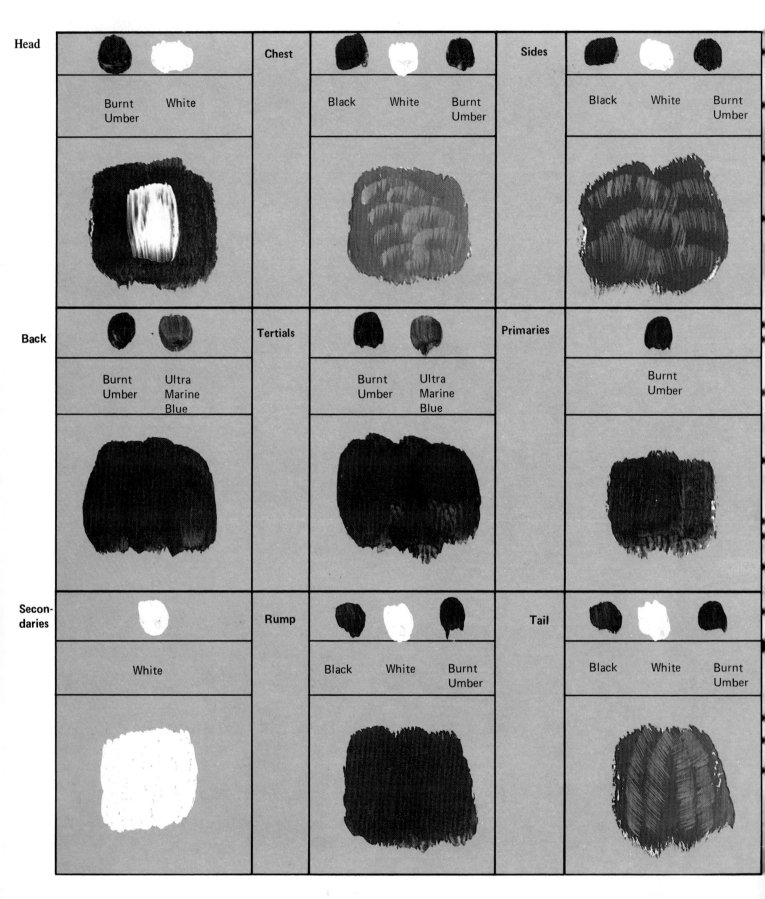

Head

Burnt Umber / White

Chest

Black / White / Burnt Umber

Sides

Black / White / Burnt Umber

Back

Burnt Umber / Ultra Marine Blue

Tertials

Burnt Umber / Ultra Marine Blue

Primaries

Burnt Umber

Secon-daries

White

Rump

Black / White / Burnt Umber

Tail

Black / White / Burnt Umber

Bufflehead hen — head and bill detail

Bufflehead hen — side and tail area

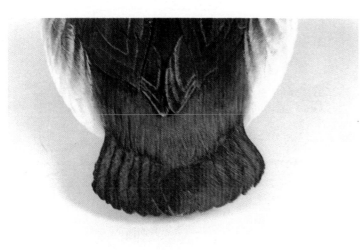

Bufflehead hen — primaries and tail detail

Bufflehead hen — crown detail

Bufflehead hen decoy by Harry Groome

Bufflehead hen decoy — side and tail area

Canvasback drake swimming

Canvasback — profile

Species: Canvas Back
Sex: Drake

PAINTING INSTRUCTIONS

Color list: *Black, White, Burnt umber, Burnt sienna, Yellow ochre, ultra-marine blue.*
Tail: brownish gray.
Underside: dusky gray, using black, white, and burnt umber.
Rump: Top and Bottom: black, using black and burnt umber or ultra-marine blue with burnt umber.
Chest: black, using ultra-marine blue and burnt umber.
Sides and Back: off-white, using white with a touch of burnt umber, vermiculated with dark gray. Wash over with white. Final wash of burnt umber.
Secondaries: a steely gray, using black and white, edged with black and trailing edged with white.
Primaries: burnt umber with touch of a white, light in the interior, dark along the edges.
Head: burnt sienna with yellow ochre, wet blended into the cheek, and black blended into the fore-cheek and crown.
Bill: black.
Feet: bluish gray with black bars.
Webs: blackish.

CANVASBACK DRAKE

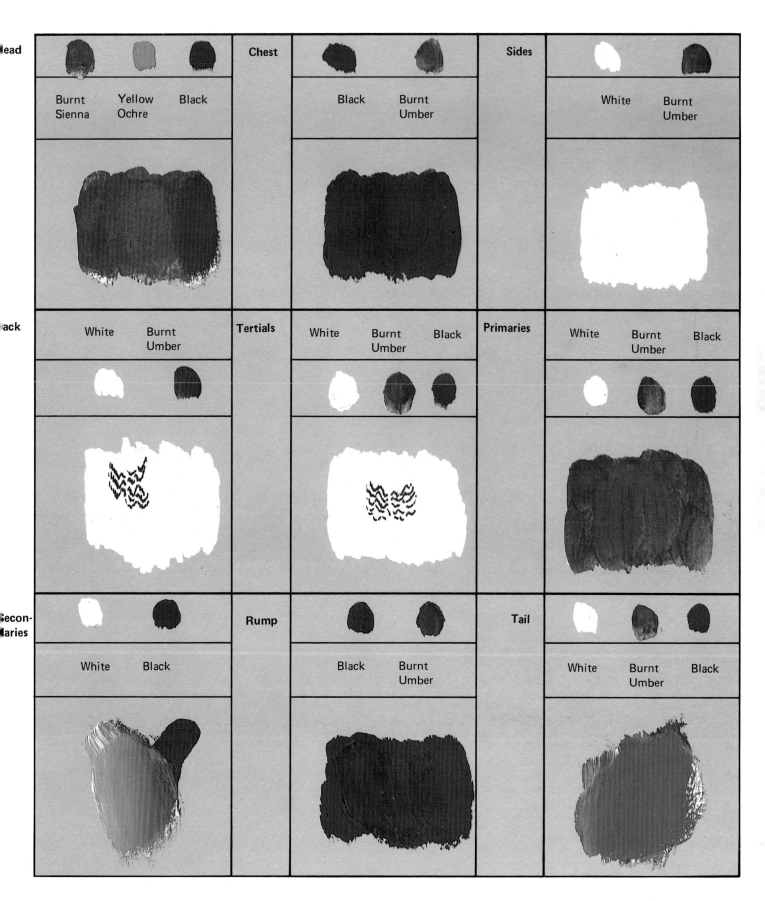

Head

Burnt Sienna   Yellow Ochre   Black

Chest

Black   Burnt Umber

Sides

White   Burnt Umber

Back

White   Burnt Umber

Tertials

White   Burnt Umber   Black

Primaries

White   Burnt Umber   Black

Secondaries

White   Black

Rump

Black   Burnt Umber

Tail

White   Burnt Umber   Black

Canvasback drake decoy by Jack Alderson

Canvasback drake decoy — head and bill detail

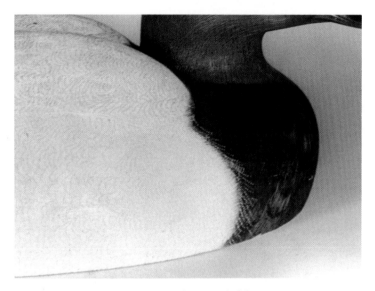

Canvasback drake decoy — chest and side area

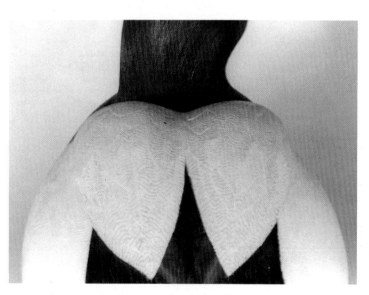

Canvasback drake decoy — back detail

Canvasback drake decoy — primaries and tail detail

Canvasback drake decoy — primaries and tail detail

Canvasback drake — bill and head detail

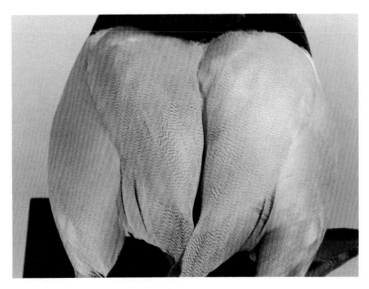
Canvasback drake — back detail

Canvasback drake — primaries and tail detail

Canvasback drake — head and neck detail

Canvasback drake – back detail

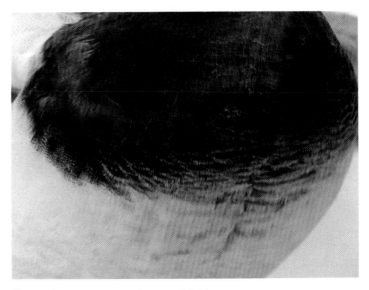
Canvasback drake — chest and belly area

Canvasback Drake

Canvasback Drake

Canvasback Drake Feeding

Canvasback Hen

Canvasback Hen

Canvasback Hen alert position

Species: Canvas Back
Sex: Hen

PAINTING INSTRUCTIONS

Color list: *Black, White, Burnt umber, Raw umber, Raw sienna.*
Tail: dusky gray, top and bottom.
Rump: brownish, using raw umber and touch of white.
Chest: raw umber with touch of white.
Sides and Back: light tan, using burnt umber and white.
All Feathers: edged with white, vermiculated with brown, washed with white several times. Final wash in burnt umber. (ultra thin)
Secondaries: steely gray, using black and white, edged with black, with faint trailing, edged with white.
Head Color: raw umber, white, and raw sienna. Burnt umber washed up the crown. Whitish around the eye and in the eye line.
Bill: dark gray, using black and white, touch of burnt umber.
Feet: bluish gray. Black bars on the toes.
Webs: blackish.

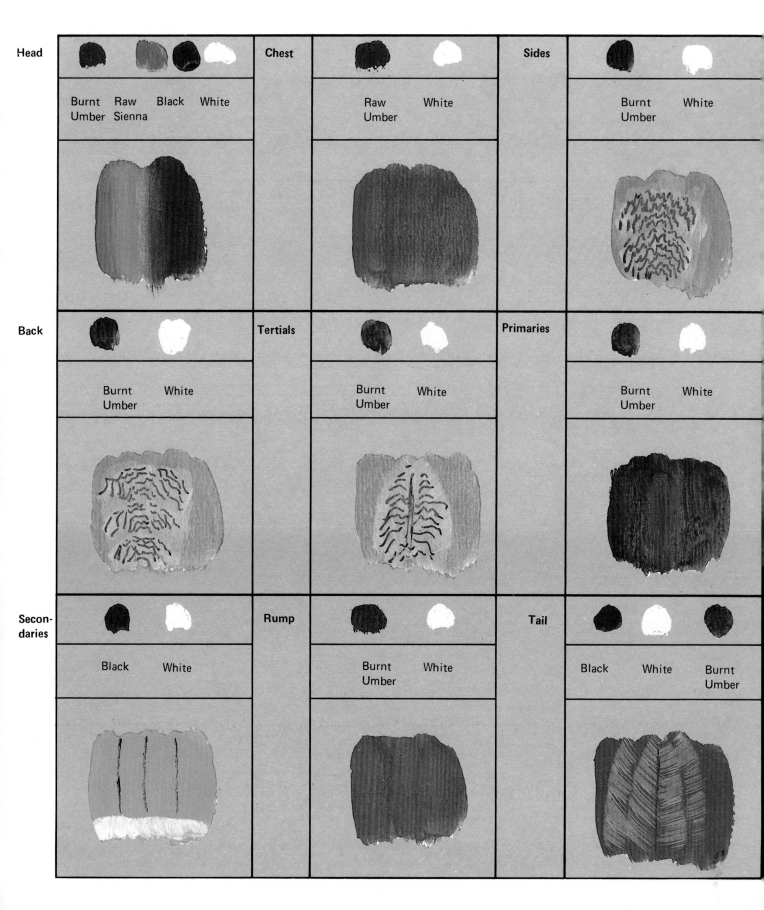

Head

Burnt Umber   Raw Sienna   Black   White

Chest

Raw Umber   White

Sides

Burnt Umber   White

Back

Burnt Umber   White

Tertials

Burnt Umber   White

Primaries

Burnt Umber   White

Secondaries

Black   White

Rump

Burnt Umber   White

Tail

Black   White   Burnt Umber

nvasback Hen decoy by Jack Alderson

Canvasback Hen — head and bill detail

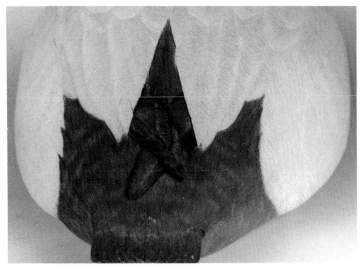

Canvasback Hen — primaries and tail detail

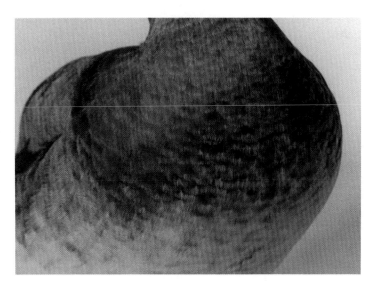

Canvasback Hen — chest detail

Canvasback Hen — back area

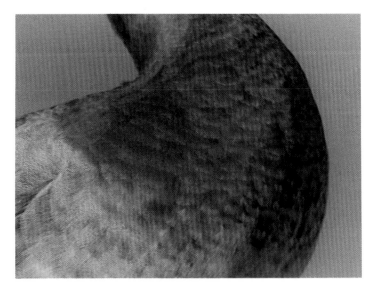

Canvasback Hen — chest and belly detail

Common Loon decorative decoy — final detail on neck

Common Loon decorative decoy — intensifying white spots on back

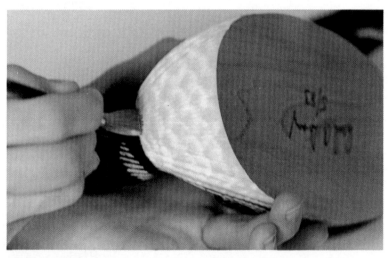

Common Loon decorative decoy — edging chest

Species: Loon
Sex: Drake and Hen
PAINTING INSTRUCTIONS

Color list: *Black, White, Burnt umber, Ultra-marine blue, Thalo green.*
Using ultra-marine blue and burnt umber, make black. Coat the back and sides of the bird with black, along water line or belly. Paint one inch line of white and dry brush a blend line; blending, white at water line to black on back.
Spots on Back, Sides and lines and Chest: white with a touc of burnt umber.
Head Color: undercoat with black. Shading cheek area with thalo green.
Bill: black to dark gray.
Feet: black.

Common Loon decorative decoy – intensifying spots on sides

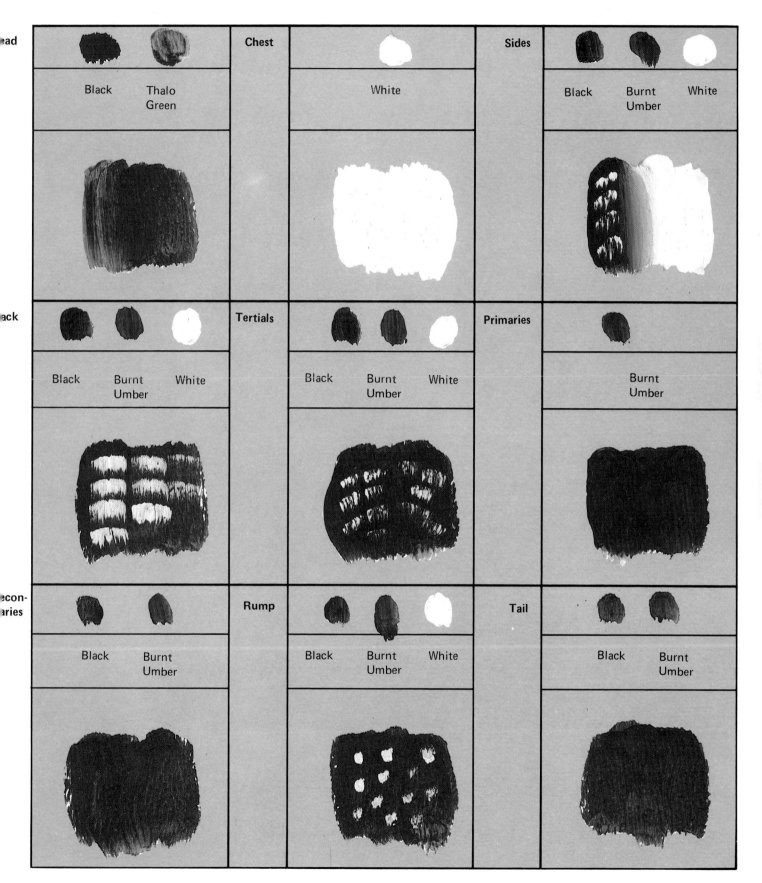

Head
Black — Thalo Green

Chest
White

Sides
Black — Burnt Umber — White

Back
Black — Burnt Umber — White

Tertials
Black — Burnt Umber — White

Primaries
Burnt Umber

Secondaries
Black — Burnt Umber

Rump
Black — Burnt Umber — White

Tail
Black — Burnt Umber

American Goldeneye hen decoy by Harry Groome

American Goldeneye Hen

American Goldeneye Hen

Species: American and Barrow's Golden-eye
Sex: Hen

PAINTING INSTRUCTIONS

Color list: *Black, White, Burnt umber, Ultra-marine blue, Raw sienna, touch of red.*
The entire body is slate gray, using black, white, and burnt umber.
Sides: edged with white. White along the belly line. Dry brush blend so that it's darker on the back and very light along the water line and belly.
Head: burnt umber.
Bill: dark gray, using black, white, and burnt umber. Touch of red, raw sienna and white for flesh color.

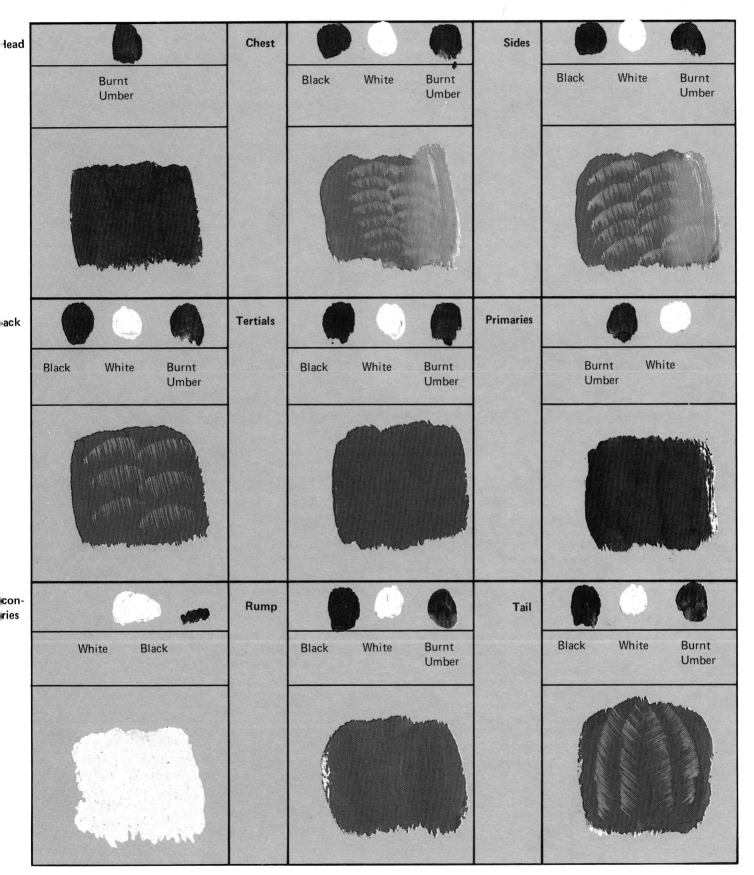

Head

Burnt
Umber

Chest

Black   White   Burnt
Umber

Sides

Black   White   Burnt
Umber

Back

Black   White   Burnt
Umber

Tertials

Black   White   Burnt
Umber

Primaries

Burnt   White
Umber

Secondaries

White   Black

Rump

Black   White   Burnt
Umber

Tail

Black   White   Burnt
Umber

American Goldeneye Hen — bill and side detail

American Goldeneye Hen decoy — head and bill detail

American Goldeneye Hen — side and tail detail

American Goldeneye Hen decoy — side, primaries and tail

American Goldeneye Hen — side area

American Goldeneye Hen — tail detail

Barrows Goldeneye Drake

Barrows Goldeneye Drake

Barrows Goldeneye Drake

Species: Barrows Golden Eye
Sex: Drake

PAINTING INSTRUCTIONS

Color list: *Black, White, Burnt umber, Yellow ochre, Thalo green, Thalo yellow-green, Thalo violet, ultra-marine blue.*
Tail: dusky gray. Top and bottom. Use black, white, and burnt umber.
Rump and Back: black and ultra-marine blue. Under rump: brownish gray.
Sides, Chest, and Neck: white, touch of burnt umber.
Secondaries: white.
Primaries: grayish, using black, white, and burnt umber.
Head: purplish with some black blended into the crown and the hooded area.
Bill: black.
Feet: yellow ochre with spots of black on the toes.
Webs: blackish.

Barrows Goldeneye Drake — head and bill detail

115

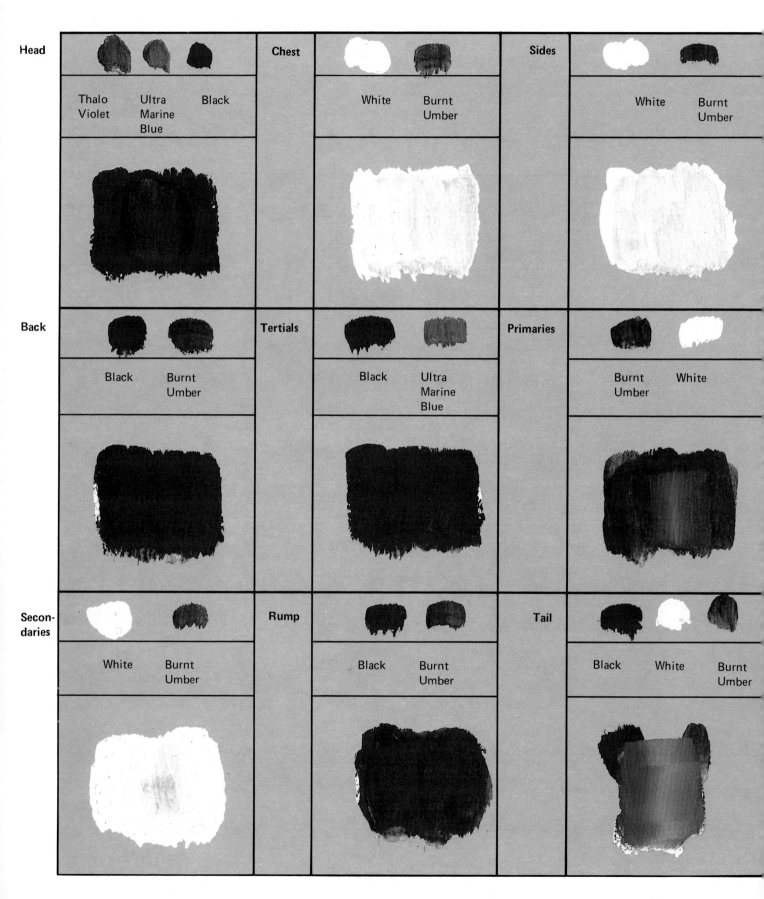

Head: Thalo Violet, Ultra Marine Blue, Black

Chest: White, Burnt Umber

Sides: White, Burnt Umber

Back: Black, Burnt Umber

Tertials: Black, Ultra Marine Blue

Primaries: Burnt Umber, White

Secondaries: White, Burnt Umber

Rump: Black, Burnt Umber

Tail: Black, White, Burnt Umber

American Goldeneye Drake

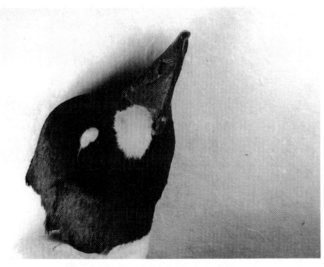

American Goldeneye Drake — head and bill detail

Species: American Golden Eye
Sex: Drake

PAINTING INSTRUCTIONS

Color list: *Black, White, Burnt umber, Yellow ochre, Thalo green, Thalo yellow-green, Thalo violet, ultra-marine blue.*
Tail: dusky gray. Top and bottom. Use black, white, and burnt umber.
Rump and Back: black and ultra-marine blue. Under rump: brownish gray.
Sides, Chest, and Neck: white, touch of burnt umber.
Secondaries: white.
Primaries: grayish brown, using a black, white, and burnt umber.
Head: thalo green with a touch of yellow-green. Some black blended into the crown and the hooded area.
Bill: black.
Feet: yellow ochre with spots of black on the toes.
Webs: blackish.

American Goldeneye — pair

117

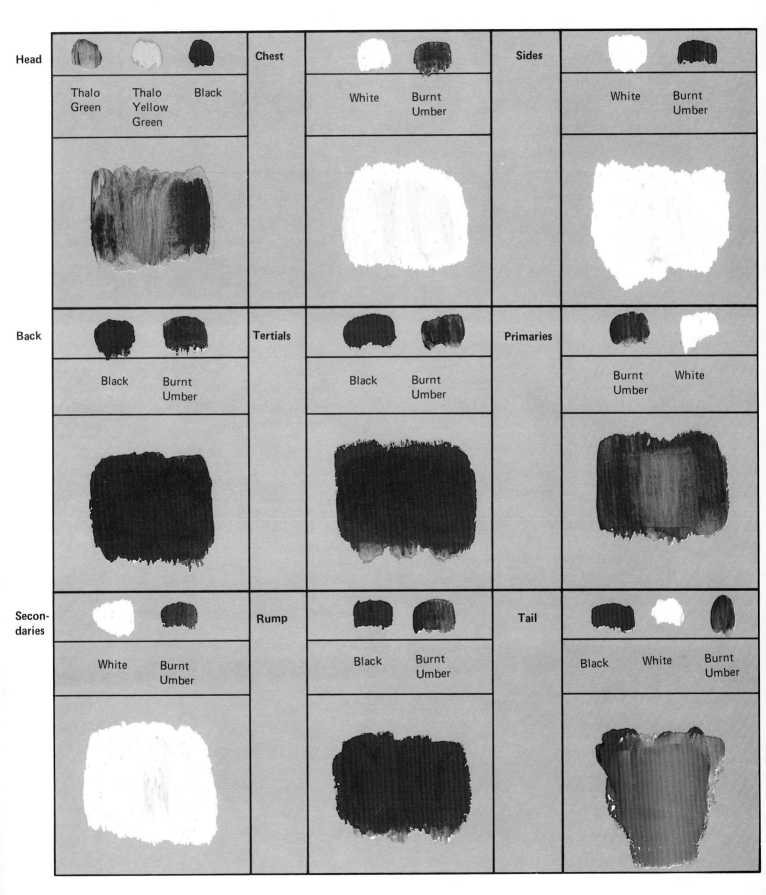

Head

Thalo Green | Thalo Yellow Green | Black

Chest

White | Burnt Umber

Sides

White | Burnt Umber

Back

Black | Burnt Umber

Tertials

Black | Burnt Umber

Primaries

Burnt Umber | White

Secondaries

White | Burnt Umber

Rump

Black | Burnt Umber

Tail

Black | White | Burnt Umber

Hooded merganser drake swimming

Hooded merganser drake swimming

Species: Hooded Merganser
Sex: Drake

PAINTING INSTRUCTIONS

Color list: *Black, White, Burnt umber, Yellow ochre, Burnt sienna.*
Tail: brownish-gray—more to the brown.
Rump: top and bottom: blackish-brown.
Sides: yellow ochre washed with a thin wash of burnt sienna, vermiculated with black.
Chest: white with two black bars.
Scapulars: whitish.
Tertials: blackish-brown, edged in white.
Inner Secondaries and Secondary Coverts: white.
Outer Secondaries and Secondary Coverts: black.
Head: black with a white patch.
Feet: yellow, using yellow ochre, with a touch of white, washed with black.
Webs: blackish.
Toes: spotted with black.
Nails: black.

Hooded merganser pair

HOODED MERGANSER DRAKE

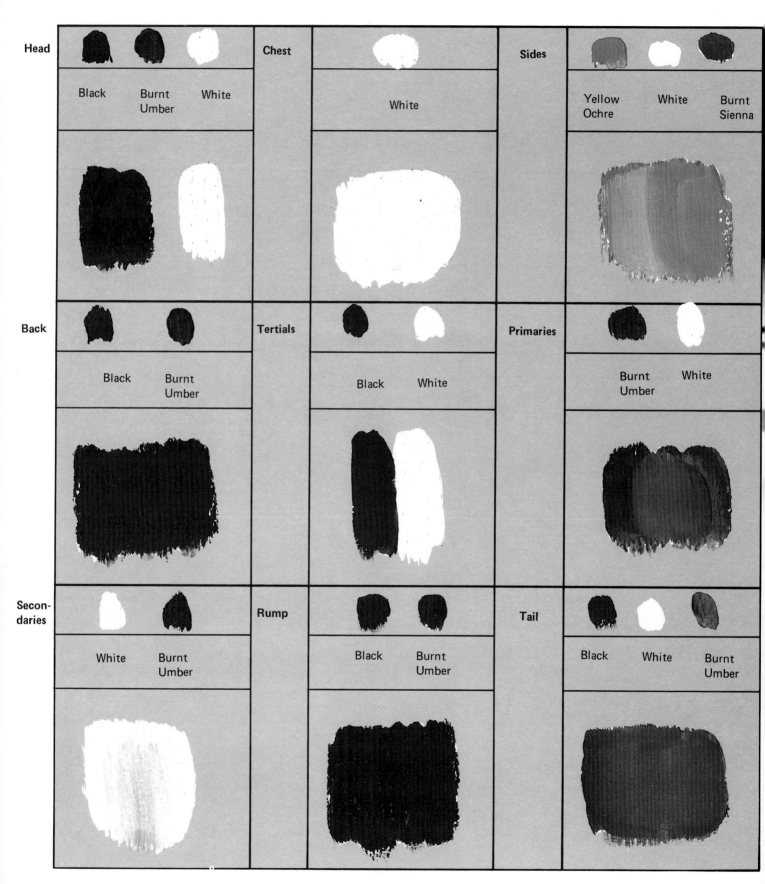

Head

Black   Burnt Umber   White

Chest

White

Sides

Yellow Ochre   White   Burnt Sienna

Back

Black   Burnt Umber

Tertials

Black   White

Primaries

Burnt Umber   White

Secondaries

White   Burnt Umber

Rump

Black   Burnt Umber

Tail

Black   White   Burnt Umber

Hooded merganser drake decorative decoy — back —
primaries, tertials and tail detail

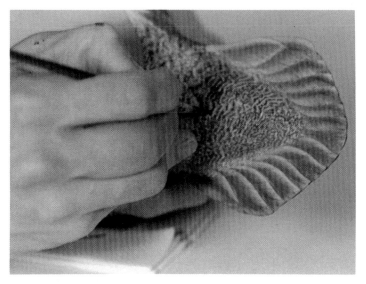

Hooded merganser drake decorative decoy — vermieculating rump

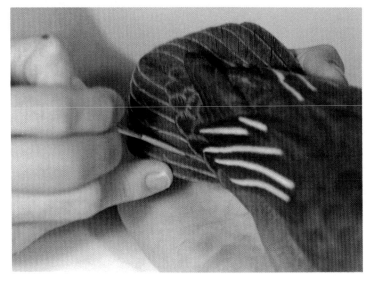

Hooded merganser drake decoy — edging tail

Hooded merganser drake decoy — final edging on crest

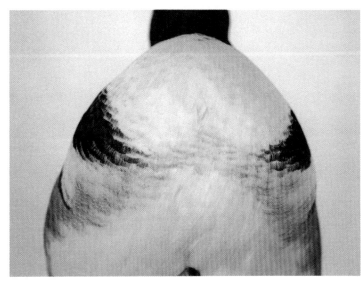

Hooded merganser drake — chest and belly area

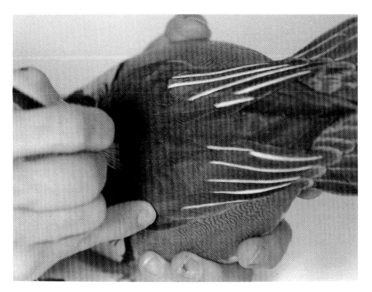

Hooded merganser drake decoy — edging back

Hooded merganser drake decoy—vermiculating sides

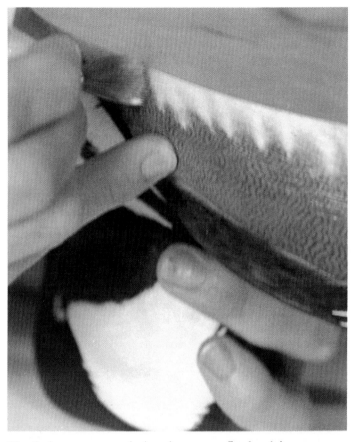

Hooded merganser drake decoy — final edging on bottom of side

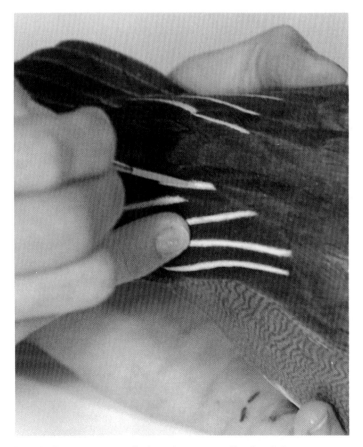

Hooded merganser drake decoy — final edging on tertials

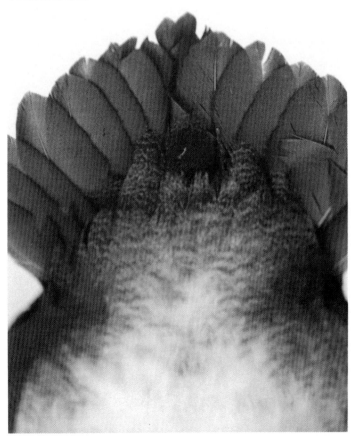

Hooded merganser drake — rump detail

Hooded Merganser Hen

Hooded merganser hen—head and chest detail

Hooded merganser hen

Species: Hooded Merganser
Sex: Hen

PAINTING INSTRUCTIONS

Color list: *Black, White, Burnt umber, Raw sienna, Burnt sienna, Yellow ochre.*
Body: brownish gray. Lighter toward the belly.
Sides: more to the brownish-gray.
Chest: more to the gray, lighter gray.
Belly: whitish.
Feathers on the Sides and Chest: edged with white.
Back: very dark brownish-gray, almost black.
Head: brownish-gray with the crest going into a buffy color, using raw sienna and white, and washed with burnt sienna for a reddish cast.
Bill: yellowish to yellow orange with a ridge, mottled with black.
Feet: same as the drake: yellowish, using yellow ochre and white.
Nail: black.

Hooded merganser hen swimming

123

HOODED MERGANSER HEN

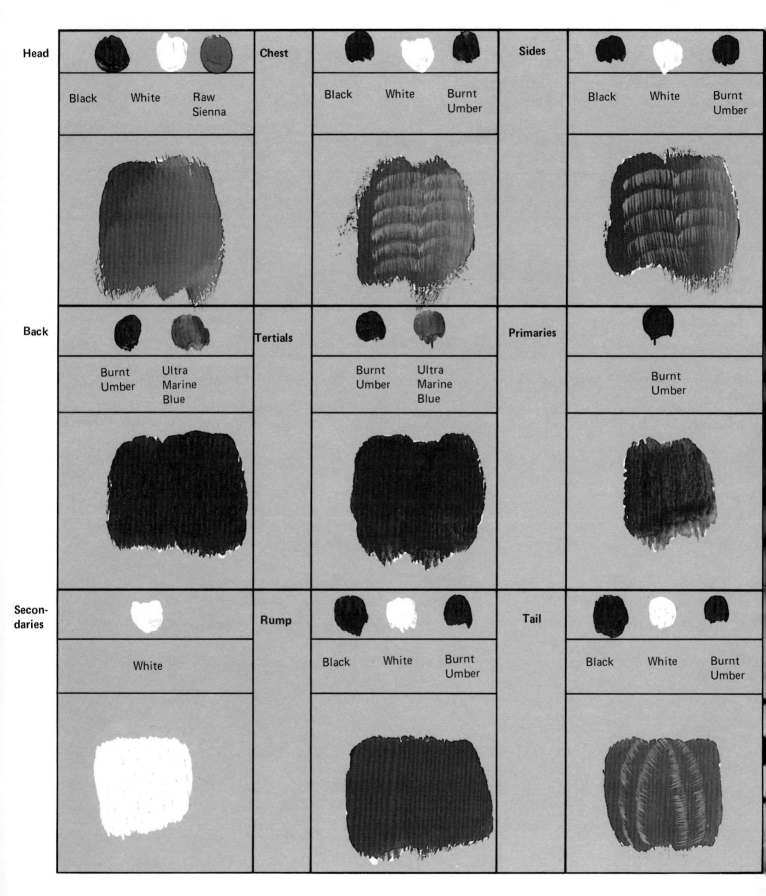

Head

Black   White   Raw Sienna

Chest

Black   White   Burnt Umber

Sides

Black   White   Burnt Umber

Back

Burnt Umber   Ultra Marine Blue

Tertials

Burnt Umber   Ultra Marine Blue

Primaries

Burnt Umber

Secondaries

White

Rump

Black   White   Burnt Umber

Tail

Black   White   Burnt Umber

Hooded merganser hen — head — cheek — bill and crest detail

Hooded merganser hen — secondaries and secondary coverts

Hooded merganser hen — crest and side area

Hooded merganser hen swimming

Red breasted merganser drake — chest and side detail

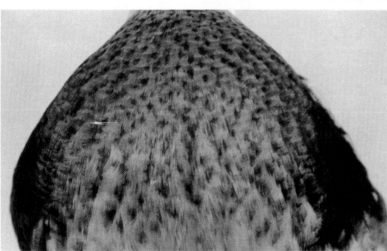

Red breasted merganser drake — chest detail

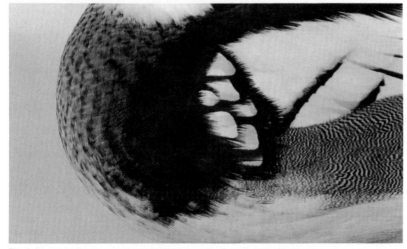

Red breasted merganser drake — chest and side detail

Species: Red-Breasted Merganser
Sex: Drake

PAINTING INSTRUCTIONS

Color list: *Black, White, Burnt umber, Burnt sienna, Raw sienna, Thalo green, Thalo yellow-green, Napthol crimson.*
Tail: gray.
Rump: gray, vermiculated with black and white.
Sides: white, vermiculated with black. Black patch with white spots between the sides and breast.
Breast Color: raw sienna, white, with a touch of burnt sienna, mottled or spotted with black.
Back and Tertials: blackish. Black mixed with burnt umber.
Primaries: burnt umber with a touch of white. There's a white patch on the neck.
Head: thalo green with a touch of yellow-green on the cheek.
Crown: washed with black.
Bill: reddish, ridge mottled with black.
Feet: reddish.
Webs: dusky.
Toes: with black spots.
Nail: black.

RED-BREASTED MERGANSER DRAKE

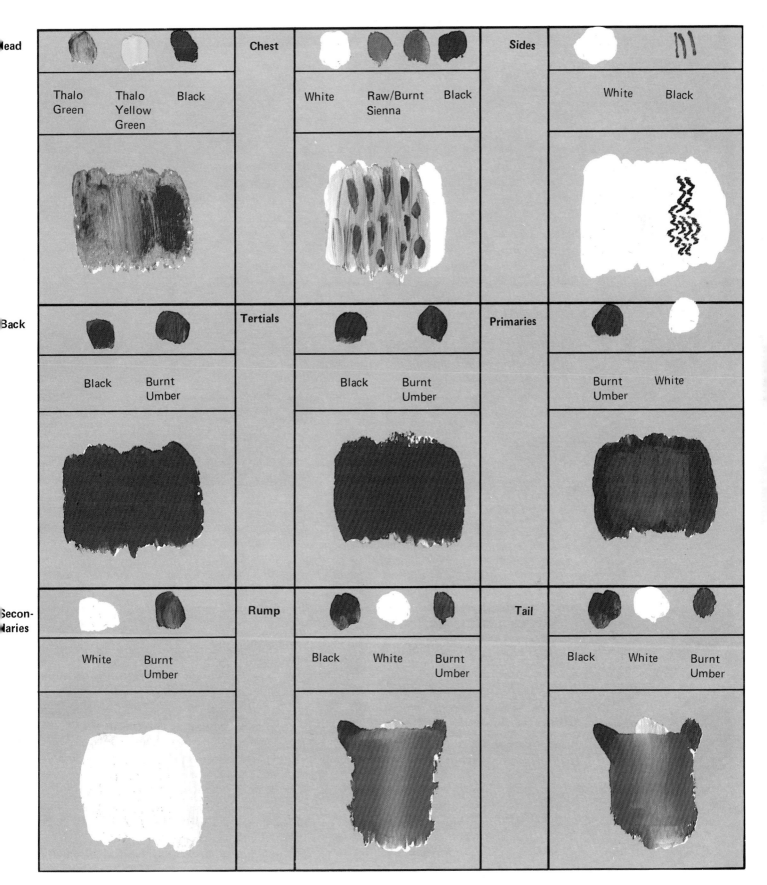

Head — Thalo Green, Thalo Yellow Green, Black	**Chest** — White, Raw/Burnt Sienna, Black	**Sides** — White, Black
Back — Black, Burnt Umber	**Tertials** — Black, Burnt Umber	**Primaries** — Burnt Umber, White
Secondaries — White, Burnt Umber	**Rump** — Black, White, Burnt Umber	**Tail** — Black, White, Burnt Umber

Red breasted drake — neck detail

Red breasted drake — side — note distinctive black and white patch

Red breasted merganser drake — rump area

Red breasted merganser drake — primaries and tail detail

Red breasted merganser drake — side — note black and white patch

Red breasted merganser drake — head — neck and bill detail

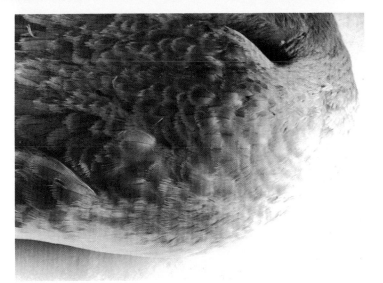

Red breasted merganser hen — chest and side detail

ed Breasted Merganser hen — cheek, bill and belly detail

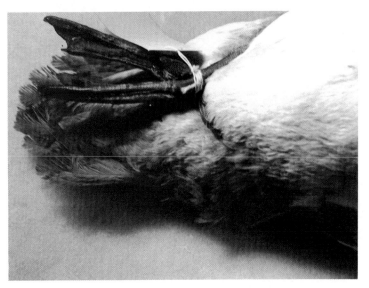

Red breasted merganser hen — belly and rump area

Species: Red-Breasted Merganser
Sex: Hen

PAINTING INSTRUCTIONS

Color list: *Black, White, Burnt umber, Burnt sienna, Raw sienna, Napthol crimson, Yellow ochre.*
Entire Body: slaty gray, using black, white, and burnt umber.
All Feathers: edged in white.
Belly: whitish.
Secondaries: inner band: white. Inner coverts: white. Outer coverts and secondaries: black and white.
Primaries: brown with a touch of white.
Head: a soft, reddish-brown, using burnt sienna, raw sienna, black and white.
Chin: whitish.
Bill: between orange and red, using red and a little bit of yellow and burnt umber, mottled down the ridge.
Feet: reddish, using yellow ochre and red.
Toes: with black spots.
Nails: black.

129

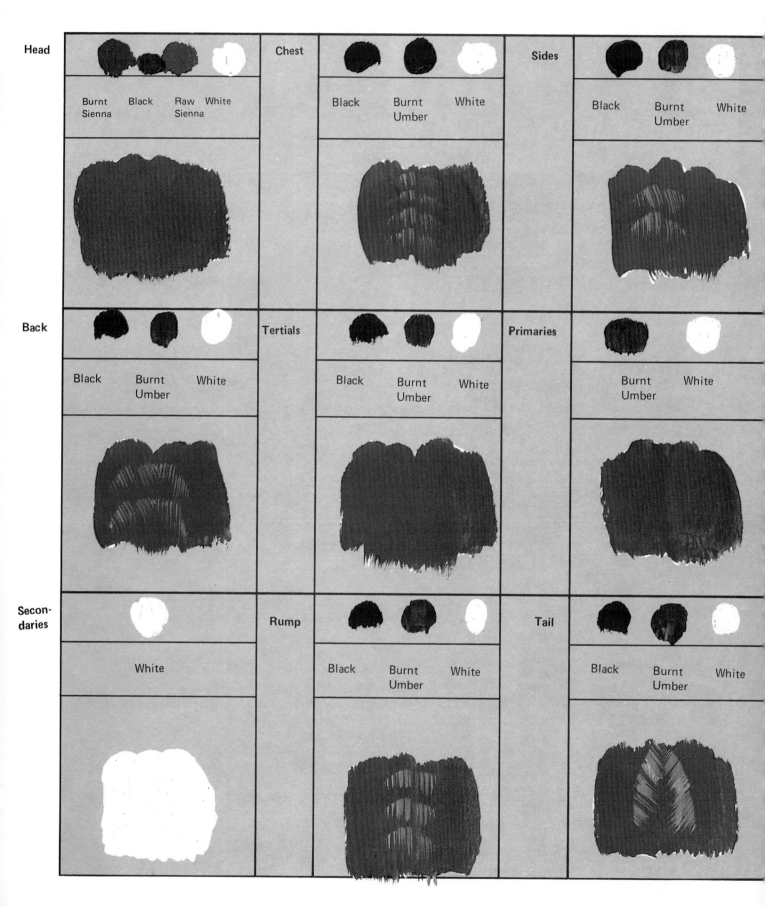

Head — Burnt Sienna, Black, Raw Sienna, White

Chest — Black, Burnt Umber, White

Sides — Black, Burnt Umber, White

Back — Black, Burnt Umber, White

Tertials — Black, Burnt Umber, White

Primaries — Burnt Umber, White

Secondaries — White

Rump — Black, Burnt Umber, White

Tail — Black, Burnt Umber, White

American Merganser Drake decoy by Anthony Christoflich

Species: American Merganser
Sex: Hen

PAINTING INSTRUCTIONS

Color list: *Black, White, Burnt umber, Raw sienna, Burnt sienna, Yellow ochre.*
Entire Body: slaty gray, using black, white, and burnt umber.
All Feathers: edged in white.
Belly: whitish.
Secondaries: inner band: white. Inner coverts: white. Outer coverts and secondaries: black.
Primaries: brown with a touch of white.
Head: a soft, reddish-brown, using burnt sienna, raw sienna, and white.
Chin: whitish.
Bill: between orange and red, using red and a little bit of yellow and burnt umber, mottled down the ridge.
Feet: reddish, using yellow ochre and red.
Toes: reddish, using yellow ochre and red; with black spots.
Nails: black.

Species: American Merganser
Sex: Drake

PAINTING INSTRUCTIONS

Color list: *Thalo green, Thalo yellow-green, Napthol Crimson, Black, White, Burnt umber, Raw sienna, Yellow ochre.*
Tail: dusky gray, edged with white.
Upper Rump Area: light dusky gray. Feathers edged in white and sometimes vermiculated with a little black and white.
Sides and Chest: white, washed with raw sienna.
Back: black, using black and burnt umber.
Scapulars: whitish.
Secondaries: white, edged with black.
Secondary Coverts: white, edged with black. Outer ones: blackish.
Primaries: burnt umber, touched with white, and washed with blackish and black on the tips.
Head: thalo green, with a touch of yellow-green, highlighted in the cheek; washed with black, darker on the crown.
Bill: red with black down the ridge and a black nail.
Feet: reddish, using yellow ochre and red.
Toes: with black spots.
Nails: black.

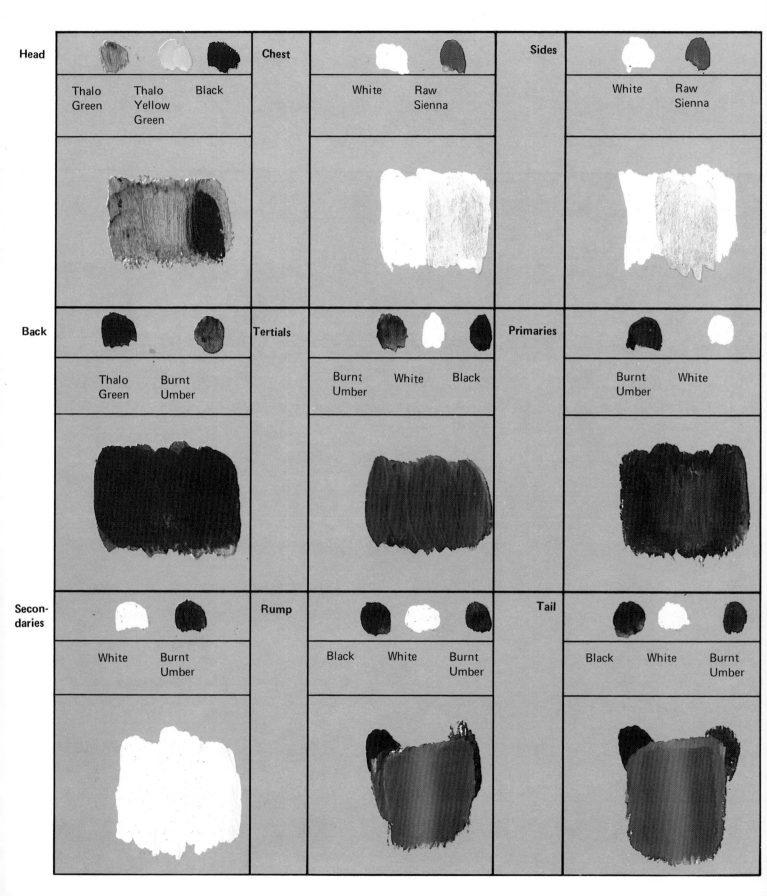

Head			Chest			Sides		
Thalo Green	Thalo Yellow Green	Black	White	Raw Sienna		White	Raw Sienna	

Back			Tertials			Primaries		
Thalo Green	Burnt Umber		Burnt Umber	White	Black	Burnt Umber	White	

Secondaries			Rump			Tail		
White	Burnt Umber		Black	White	Burnt Umber	Black	White	Burnt Umber

AMERICAN MERGANSER HEN

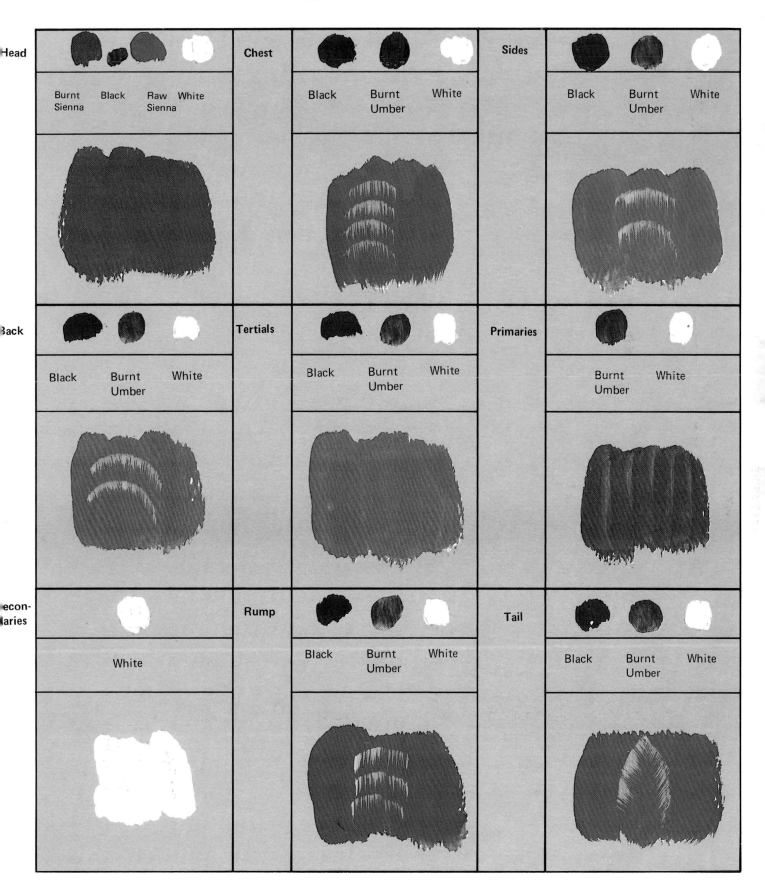

Head — Burnt Sienna, Black, Raw Sienna, White

Chest — Black, Burnt Umber, White

Sides — Black, Burnt Umber, White

Back — Black, Burnt Umber, White

Tertials — Black, Burnt Umber, White

Primaries — Burnt Umber, White

Secondaries — White

Rump — Black, Burnt Umber, White

Tail — Black, Burnt Umber, White

Ringed necked duck drake — profile

Ring necked duck drake — crest — head and bill area

Ring necked duck drake — blending bill

Species: Ring Neck
Sex: Drake

PAINTING INSTRUCTIONS

Color list: *Black, White, Burnt umber, Payne's gray, Thalo violet, Thalo green, Burnt sienna.*

Upper Tail: brownish gray, using black, white, and burnt umber.

Under Tail: dusky gray. Both colors made with black, white, and burnt umber. More burnt umber on the upper side.

Rump and under Rump: black with burnt umber.

Sides and Belly: whitish. There's a bluish-black vermiculation through the sides.

Back and Chest: black with burnt umber. Some thalo green blended into the back.

Secondaries: steely gray blended into brown, and trailing edge is white.

Primaries: burnt umber, touch of white, lighter in the interior. Dark edges.

Head: black with thalo violet blended into the cheek and crest areas. There's a faint, burnt sienna ring about ¼ an inch wide around the neck.

Bill: Payne's gray and white, touched with burnt umber, a white band, and black tip.

Feet: grayish with black bands and toes.

Webs: blackish.

RING-NECKED DUCK DRAKE

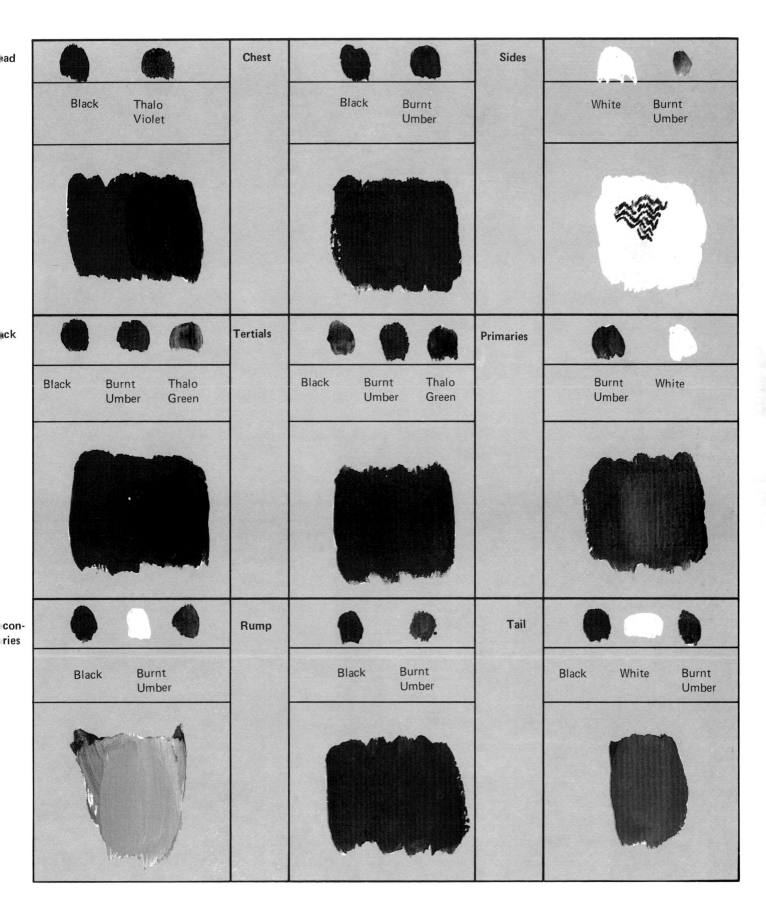

Head		Chest		Sides	
Black	Thalo Violet	Black	Burnt Umber	White	Burnt Umber

Back			Tertials			Primaries	
Black	Burnt Umber	Thalo Green	Black	Burnt Umber	Thalo Green	Burnt Umber	White

Secon-daries			Rump		Tail		
Black	Burnt Umber		Black	Burnt Umber	Black	White	Burnt Umber

Ring neck duck

Ring neck duck decorative decoy by Sandy Stromberg

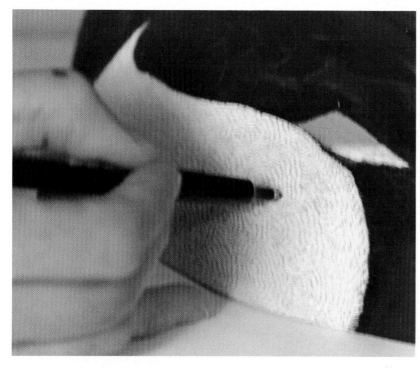

Ring neck duck decorative decoy — vermiculating sides

Ring neck duck — chest detail

Ring necked duck hen — head cheek and bill detail

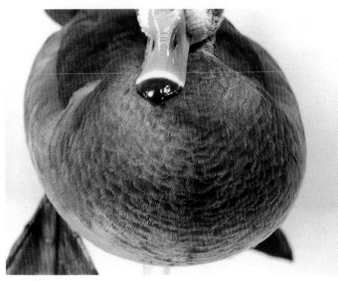

Ring necked duck hen — chest detail

Ring necked duck hen — primaries and tail detail

Ring necked duck hen —
side secondaries and tail area

Species: Ring Neck
Sex: Hen

PAINTING INSTRUCTIONS

Color list: *Burnt umber, Raw umber, White, Black, Payne's gray, Raw sienna, Yellow ochre.*
Tail: upper side brownish gray, tipped with white. Washed down under side: dusky gray, using black, white, and burnt umber.
Underside: burnt umber with white, edged with white.
Rump: burnt umber with a touch of white, edged with white.
Sides: raw umber with touch of white and yellow ochre.
Chest: edged with white and raw sienna .
Sides and Chest: raw umber and white, edged with white, with some faint vermiculations washed down.
Back: burnt umber, edged with white and vermiculated faintly with white specks.
Secondaries: pearly gray with trailing edges of white. Pearly gray: blend black, white, and touch of burnt umber.
Head: **Base color**: raw umber and white, with touch of raw sienna. Whitish around the eye. Burnt umber with a touch of black blended into crown. White blended into the fore-cheek.
Bill: Payne's gray, white, burnt umber, white band, and black tip.
Feet: medium gray.
Webs: blackish.

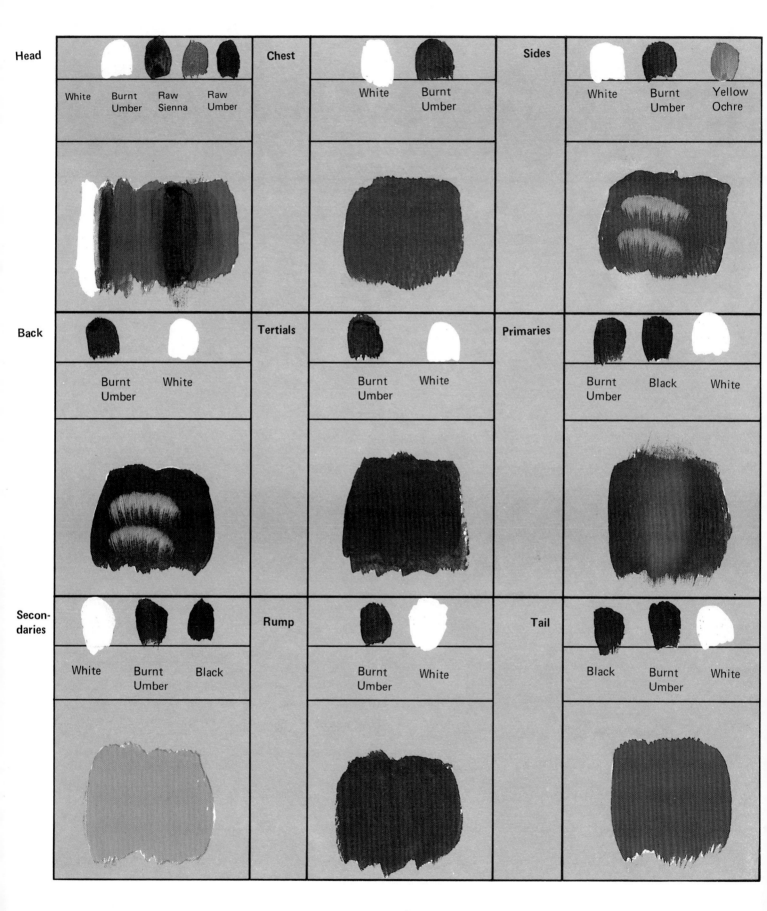

Head

White   Burnt Umber   Raw Sienna   Raw Umber

Chest

White   Burnt Umber

Sides

White   Burnt Umber   Yellow Ochre

Back

Burnt Umber   White

Tertials

Burnt Umber   White

Primaries

Burnt Umber   Black   White

Secondaries

White   Burnt Umber   Black

Rump

Burnt Umber   White

Tail

Black   Burnt Umber   White

Old squaw drake — tail detail

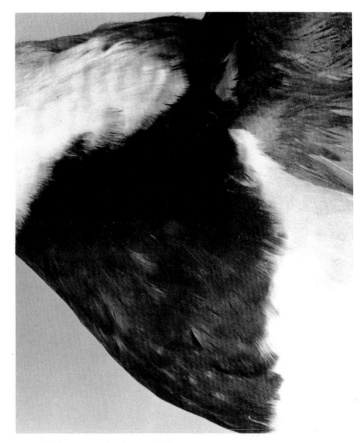

Old squaw drake — side area

Old squaw drake — top view wing area

Squaw drake — under wing detail

Species: Old Squaw
Sex: Hen

PAINTING INSTRUCTIONS

Color list: *Black, White, Burnt umber, Raw sienna, Burnt umber.*
Tail, Sides: brown, using burnt umber and white, edged with white.
Back and Upper Chest Feathers: burnt umber, edged with raw sienna and white.
Belly: white.

Secondaries: brown.
Primaries: brown; use burnt umber, touched with white, light on the inside.
Head: whitish with a dark brown, almost blackish crown, and dark eyeline. Burnt umber with a little black in it. Dark mark on the cheek: burnt umber with a little black in it.
Bill: grayish to flesh color, depending on the moult.
Feet: bluish gray—(Payne's gray and white) webs dusky.

139

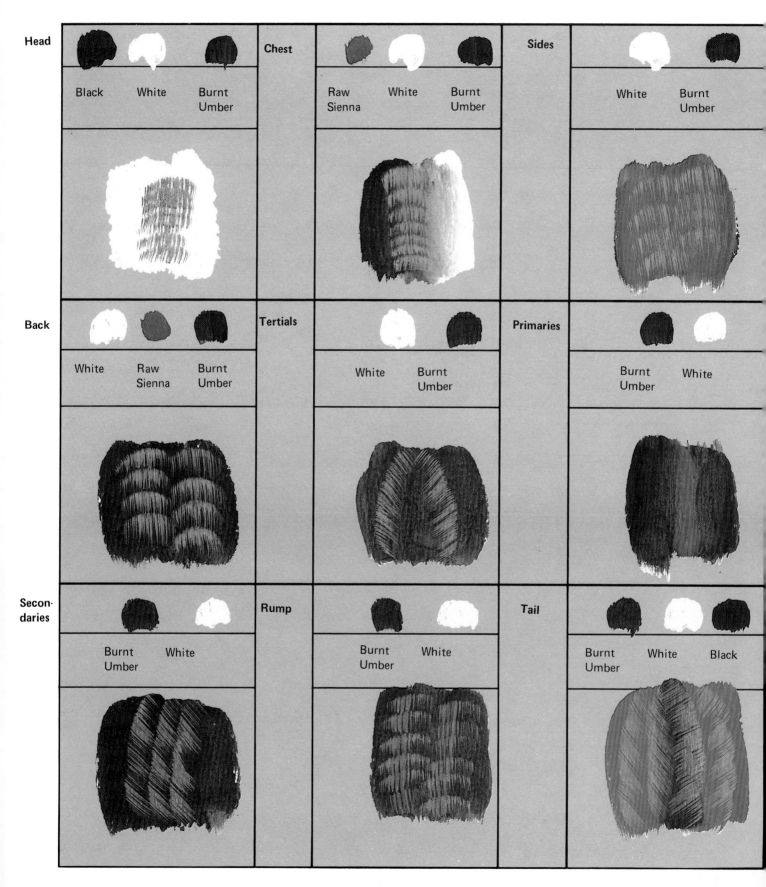

Head

Black   White   Burnt Umber

Chest

Raw Sienna   White   Burnt Umber

Sides

White   Burnt Umber

Back

White   Raw Sienna   Burnt Umber

Tertials

White   Burnt Umber

Primaries

Burnt Umber   White

Secondaries

Burnt Umber   White

Rump

Burnt Umber   White

Tail

Burnt Umber   White   Black

Old squaw drake — in flight position

Species: Old Squaw
Sex: Drake

PAINTING INSTRUCTIONS

Color list: *Black, White, Burnt umber, Red, Raw sienna.*
Tail: gray edged with white. Blend black and burnt umber all the way up the center of the back, feeding into the chest color, which is also black mixed with burnt umber.
Back: **scapulars and tertials**: gray, using black, white, and burnt umber to mix the light gray, and edged with white.
Primaries: gray-brown, using black, white, and burnt umber. Exception: center feather, which is black.
Crown, Crest, Neck, and Throat: white, and two brown patches on the head. The light patch is a light brown, using burnt umber and white, and a dark brown patch, using burnt umber.
Bill: black, going into pink near the nail, using red, white, and raw sienna to make the pink.
Feet: grayish with black bars on the toes.
Webs: blackish.

141

OLD SQUAW DRAKE

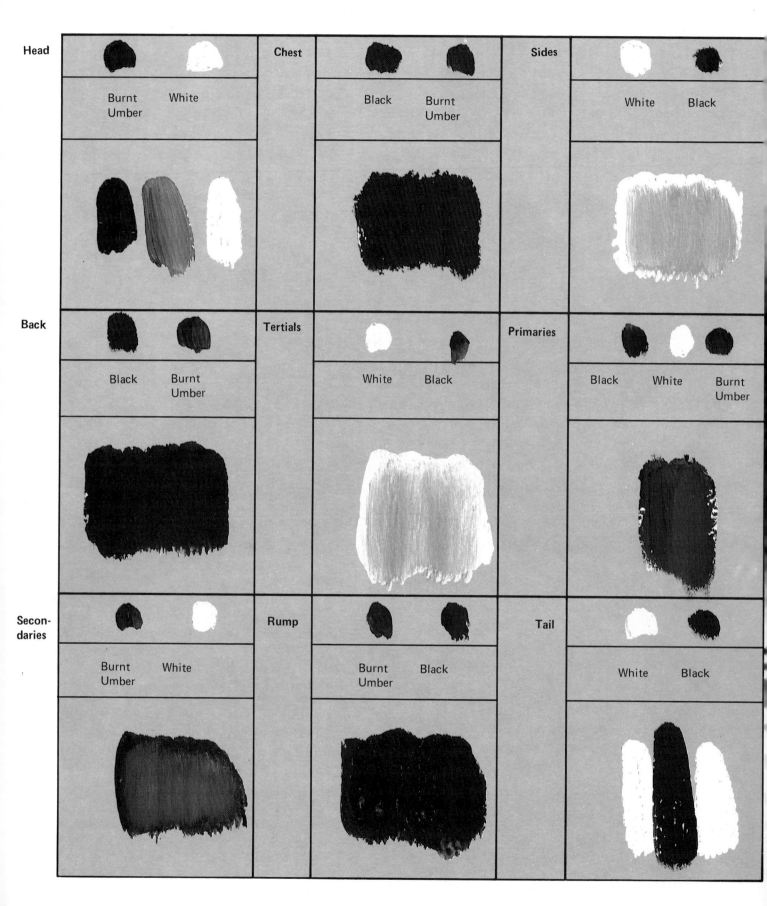

Head		Chest		Sides	
Burnt Umber	White	Black	Burnt Umber	White	Black

Back		Tertials		Primaries		
Black	Burnt Umber	White	Black	Black	White	Burnt Umber

Secondaries		Rump		Tail	
Burnt Umber	White	Burnt Umber	Black	White	Black

Red Head Drake sleeper decoy by Sina "Pat" Kurman

Red Head Drake

Red Head Drake

Species: Red Head
Sex: Drake

PAINTING INSTRUCTIONS

Color list: *Black, White, Burnt umber, Burnt sienna, Raw sienna, Yellow ochre, Payne's gray, Thalo violet.*
Tail: dusty gray; use black, white, and burnt umber, edged lightly with white.
Underside of Tail: light gray.
Rump, along the Rump: black with burnt umber.
Sides: under coat with off-white, using white mixed with a touch of burnt umber, vermiculated with black.
Chest: black with burnt umber.
Belly: whitish.
Secondaries: pearly gray, faint tips with white.
Primaries: burnt umber with touch of white.
Head Color: burnt sienna, raw sienna, thalo violet, and yellow ochre highlighting for cheek.
Bill: Payne's gray and white, for a bluish gray, white band and black tip.
Feet and Legs: dark gray with black bands.
Webs: blackish.

143

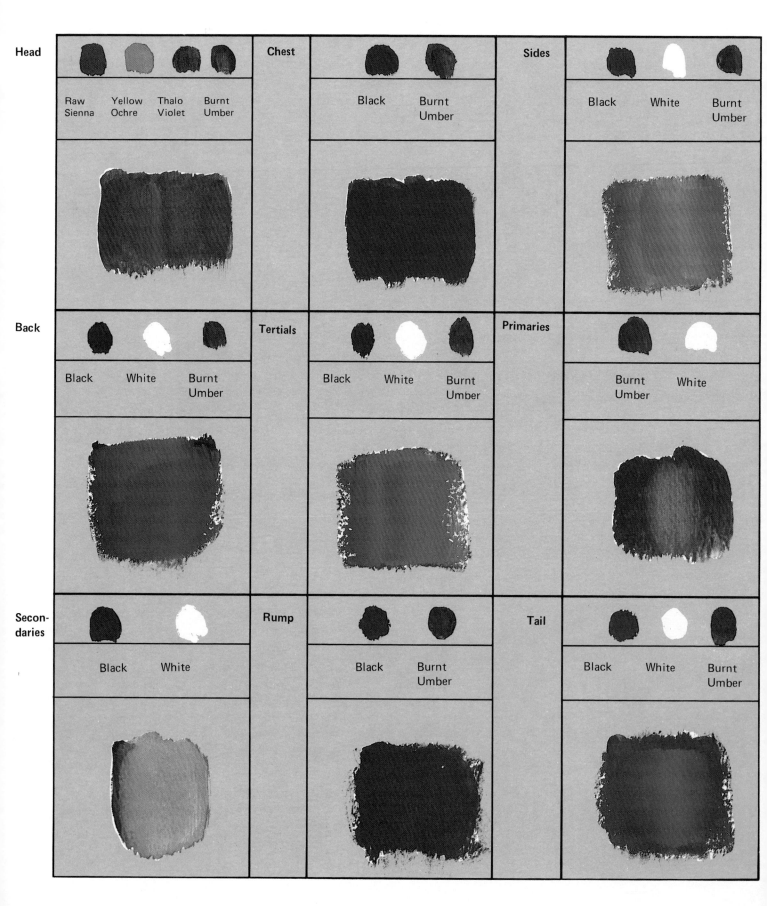

Head

Raw Sienna · Yellow Ochre · Thalo Violet · Burnt Umber

Chest

Black · Burnt Umber

Sides

Black · White · Burnt Umber

Back

Black · White · Burnt Umber

Tertials

Black · White · Burnt Umber

Primaries

Burnt Umber · White

Secondaries

Black · White

Rump

Black · Burnt Umber

Tail

Black · White · Burnt Umber

Red Head Drake decoy by Sina "Pat" Kurman

Red Head Drake — head and bill detail

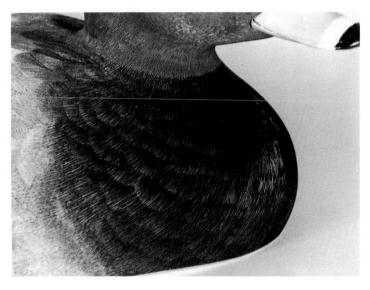

Red Head Drake — chest and side area

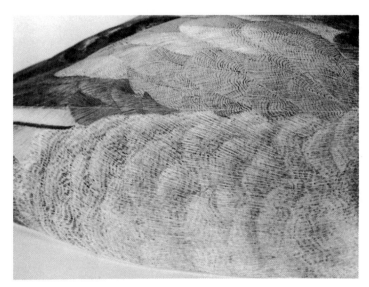

Red Head Drake — side detail

Red Head Drake — side and tail detail

Red Head Drake — primaries and tail detail

Red Head Drake — sleeper head and back detail

Red Head Drake — sleeper neck and chest area

Red Head Drake — side area

Red Head Drake — primaries tail area

Red Head Hen

Red Head Hen

Species: Red Head
Sex: Hen

PAINTING INSTRUCTIONS

Color list: *Burnt umber, Raw umber, White, Black, Payne's gray, Yellow ochre, Raw sienna.*

Tail: upper side brownish gray, tipped with white. Washed down under side: dusky gray, using black, white, and burnt umber.

Rump: burnt umber with a touch of white, edged with white.

Underside: burnt umber with white, edged with white.

Sides: raw umber with a touch of white and yellow ochre.

Chest: edged with white and raw sienna.

Sides and Chest: raw umber and white, edged with white, with some faint vermiculations brown and white washed down.

Back: burnt umber, edged with white and vermiculated faintly with white specks.

Secondaries: pearly gray with trailing edges of white. Pearly gray: blend black, white, and touch of burnt umber.

Head: **Base color**: raw umber and white, with touch of raw sienna. Whitish around the eye. Burnt umber with a touch of black blended into crown.

Bill: Payne's gray and white. A little burnt umber, white band, and black tip.

Feet: medium gray.

Webs: blackish.

Red Head Hen

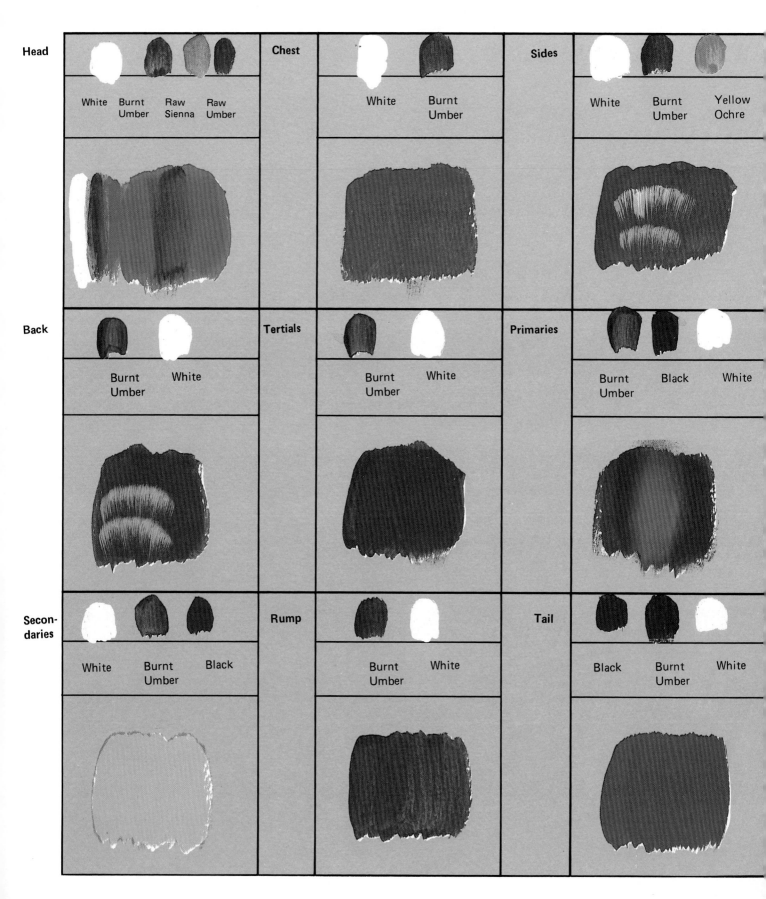

Red head hen mount

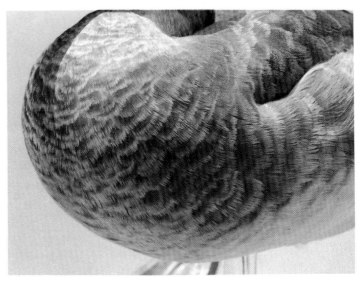

Red head hen mount—chest detail

Red head hen mount—secondaries, tertials and tail detail

Red head hen mount—side detail

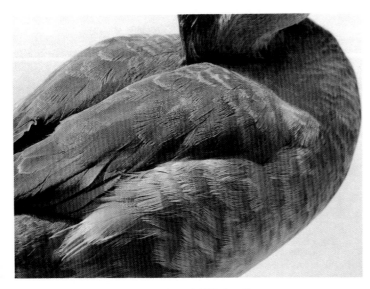

Red head hen mount—head and bill detail

Red head hen mount

Ruddy Duck Drake

Ruddy Duck Drake

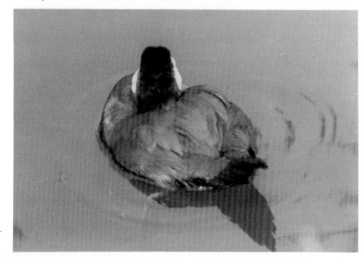

Ruddy Duck Drake

Species: Ruddy Duck
Sex: Drake

PAINTING INSTRUCTIONS

Color list: *Black, White, Burnt umber, Raw umber, Payne's gray, Burnt sienna, Yellow ochre.*
Feather Edges: gray.
Sides, Back, and Upper Chest: burnt sienna, with a touch of yellow ochre.
Back: dark, dark brown, using burnt umber and raw umber with vermiculations of white and yellowish.
Head: dark brown, with flecks of white through it.
Cheek Patch: white.
Bill: Payne's gray, white, and burnt umber.
Feet: Bluish gray—dusky webs—use Payne's gray and white. Add burnt umber to web area.

RUDDY DUCK DRAKE

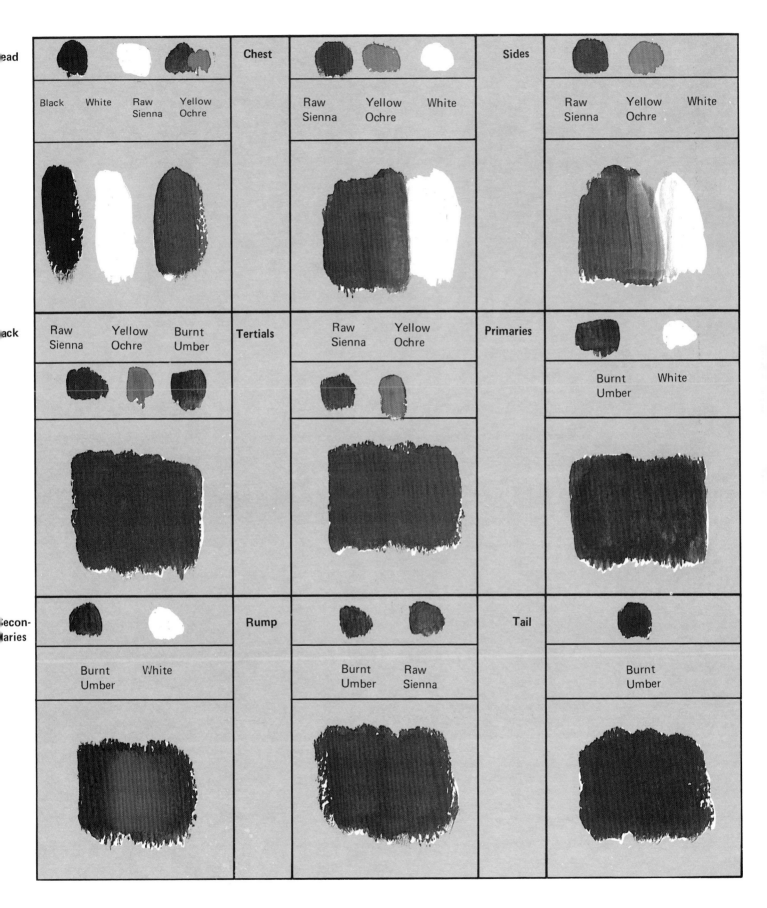

ead

| Black | White | Raw Sienna | Yellow Ochre |

Chest

| Raw Sienna | Yellow Ochre | White |

Sides

| Raw Sienna | Yellow Ochre | White |

ack

| Raw Sienna | Yellow Ochre | Burnt Umber |

Tertials

| Raw Sienna | Yellow Ochre |

Primaries

| Burnt Umber | White |

Secon- aries

| Burnt Umber | White |

Rump

| Burnt Umber | Raw Sienna |

Tail

| Burnt Umber |

151

Ruddy Drake note tail position

Ruddy Drake

Ruddy Drake

Ruddy Drake

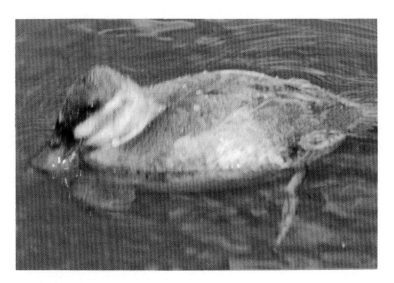

Ruddy Duck Hen

Species: Ruddy Duck
Sex: Hen

PAINTING INSTRUCTIONS

Color list: *Black, White, Burnt umber, Payne's gray, Burnt sienna, Yellow ochre, Raw umber.*
Feather Edges: gray.
Sides: silvery base, using black, white, and burnt umber; mostly white and just a dot of black. Then washed with yellow ochre, mottled with burnt umber.
Back: dark, dark brown, using burnt umber and raw umber with vermiculations of white and yellowish.
Head: dark brown, with flecks of white through it.
Cheek Patch: white. Dark streak through the white patch.
Bill: darker than the male, using Payne's gray, white, and burnt umber.

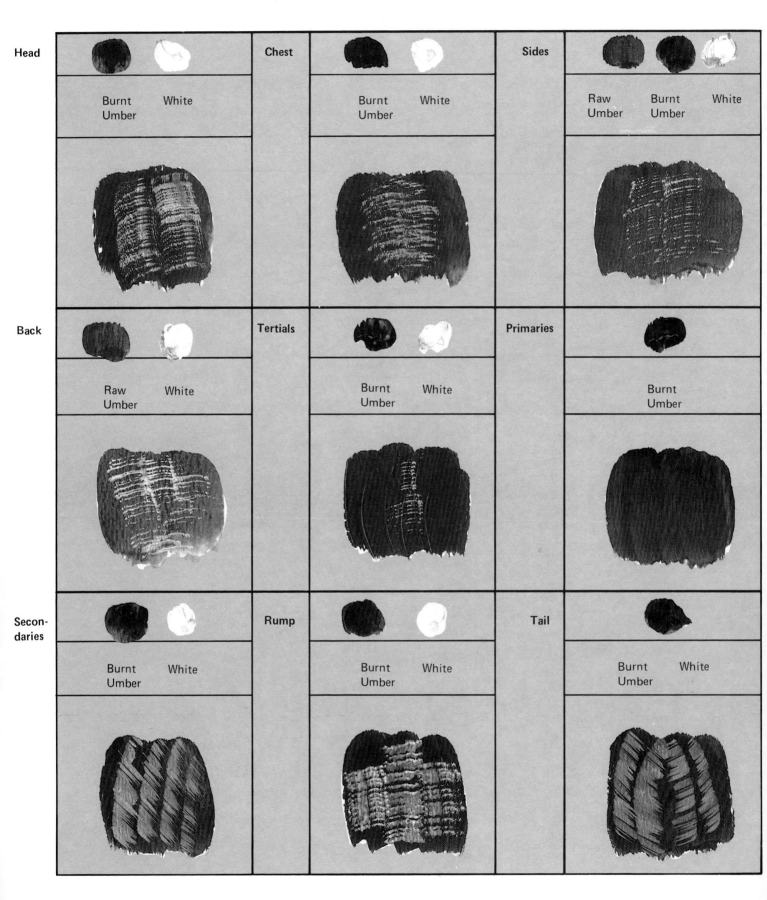

Head — Burnt Umber · White

Chest — Burnt Umber · White

Sides — Raw Umber · Burnt Umber · White

Back — Raw Umber · White

Tertials — Burnt Umber · White

Primaries — Burnt Umber

Secondaries — Burnt Umber · White

Rump — Burnt Umber · White

Tail — Burnt Umber · White

Lesser Scaup Drake

Lesser Scaup Drake — head and bill detail

Lesser Scaup Drake — side and tail area

Species: Greater Scaup
Sex: Drake

PAINTING INSTRUCTIONS

Color list: *Black, White, Burnt umber, Thalo green, Thalo yellow-green, Payne's Gray.*
Tail: dusky gray, edged with white, faintly.
Rump and under Rump: black mixed with burnt umber.
Chest: black mixed with burnt umber.
Base color: Sides and Back: white with small amount of burnt umber, vermiculated with black.
Secondaries: white; trailing edge brown. Burnt umber with touch of white, lighter in the center, darker on the outside.
Head color: thalo green, touch of yellow-green on the cheek, fore-cheek, crown, back of neck. Wet blended with black.
Bill: light bluish-gray, using Payne's gray and white.
Feet: medium gray.
Webs: blackish.
Toes: spotted with black.
Nail: black.

Note: for painting the Lesser Scaup Drake, the only difference is in the head color, the Greater Scaup being greenish and the Lesser Scaup being purplish.

GREATER SCAUP DRAKE

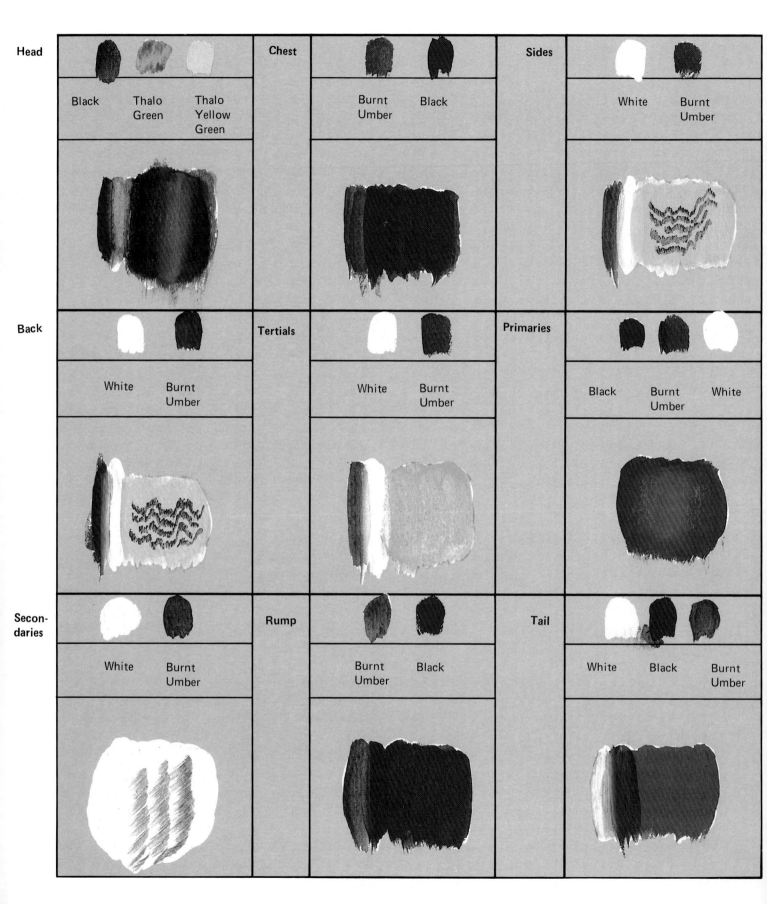

Head			Chest		Sides	
Black	Thalo Green	Thalo Yellow Green	Burnt Umber	Black	White	Burnt Umber

Back		Tertials		Primaries		
White	Burnt Umber	White	Burnt Umber	Black	Burnt Umber	White

Secondaries		Rump		Tail		
White	Burnt Umber	Burnt Umber	Black	White	Black	Burnt Umber

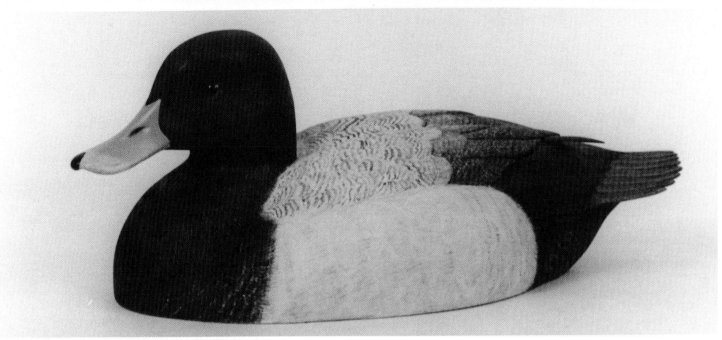

Lesser Scaup Drake decoy by Jack Alderson

Greater Scaup — Pair

Greater Scaup drake —
back — side and chest detail

Lesser scaup decoy — head and bill detail

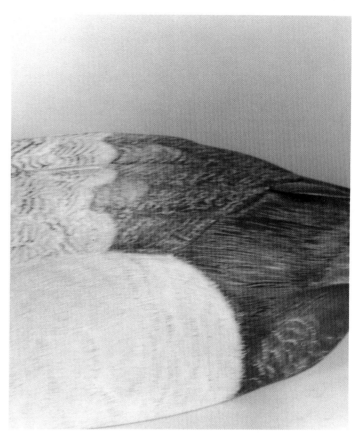

Lesser scaup decoy — side and tail area

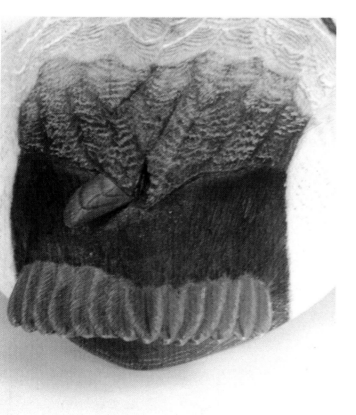

Lesser scaup decoy — primaries and tail

Species: Greater and Lesser Scaup
Sex: Hen

PAINTING INSTRUCTIONS

Color list: *Burnt umber, Raw umber, White, Black, Payne's gray, Yellow ochre, Raw sienna.*
Tail: upper side brownish gray, tipped with white. Washed down under side: dusky gray, using black, white, and burnt umber.
Underside: burnt umber with white, edged with white.
Rump: burnt umber with a touch of white, edged with white.
Sides: raw umber with touch of white and yellow ochre.
Chest: raw umber with touch of white (darker than sides).
Sides and Chest: edged with white, with some faint vermiculations washed down.
Back: burnt umber with touch of white, edged with white and vermiculated faintly with white specks.
Secondaries: pearly gray with trailing edges of white. Pearly gray: blend black, white, and touch of burnt umber.
Head: Base color: raw umber and white, with touch of raw sienna. Densely whitish around the eye, the mask area, and the fore-crown. Burnt umber with a touch of black blended into crown.
Bill: Payne's gray and white. A little burnt umber, white band, and black tip.
Feet: medium gray.
Webs: blackish.

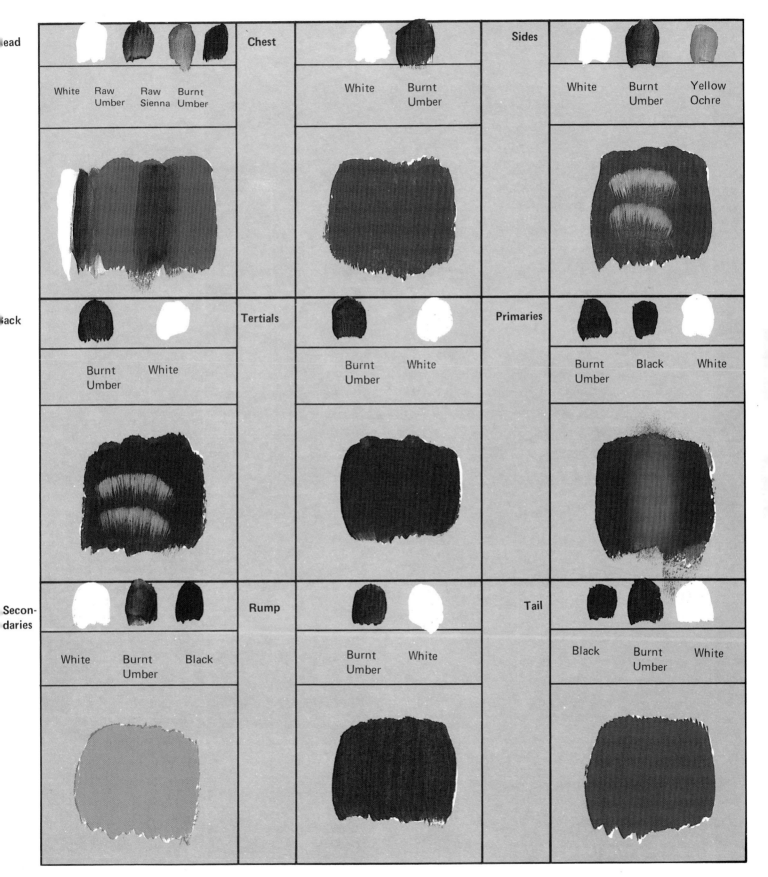

Head

White   Raw Umber   Raw Sienna   Burnt Umber

Chest

White   Burnt Umber

Sides

White   Burnt Umber   Yellow Ochre

Back

Burnt Umber   White

Tertials

Burnt Umber   White

Primaries

Burnt Umber   Black   White

Secondaries

White   Burnt Umber   Black

Rump

Burnt Umber   White

Tail

Black   Burnt Umber   White

Ring necked duck hunting decoy by Bill Veasey from collection of Dr. Marshall Sasser

Ring neck duck hunting decoy — head and bill detail

Ring neck duck hunting decoy — back area detail

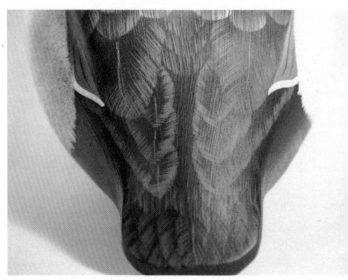

Ring neck duck hunting decoy — primaries and tail detail

Ring neck duck hunting decoy — side detail

Pintail hunting decoy by Claude Dohl, from the collection of Joe Kline

Pintail hunting decoy — cheek and bill detail

Pintail hunting decoy — side area

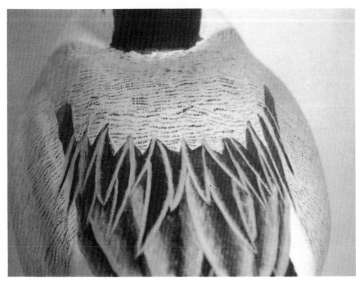

Pintail hunting decoy — back detail

Pintail hunting decoy — tertials, primaries and tail area

Canvasback hunting decoy by John Floyd

Canvasback hunting decoy — head, bill and cheek detail

Canvasback hunting decoy — primaries, secondaries, coverts

Canvasback hunting decoy — primaries, tertials, coverts and tail

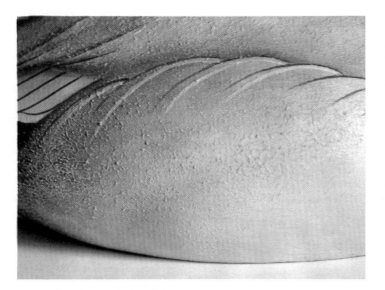

Canvasback hunting decoy — side area

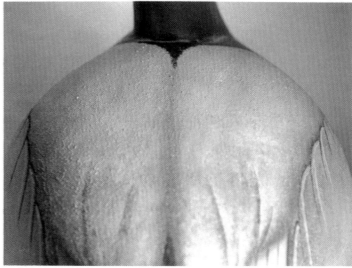

Canvasback hunting decoy — back detail

Canvasback hunting decoy by Jan Calvert, copy of a 1936 Ward

Canvasback hunting decoy — head and bill detail

Canvasback hunting decoy—tail area

Canvasback hunting decoy—side area

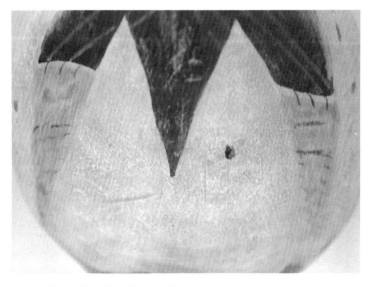

Canvasback hunting decoy—back area

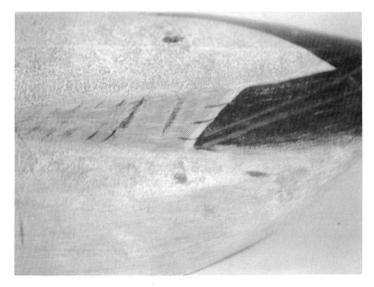

Canvasback hunting decoy—side and rump area

Green winged teal drake hunting decoy by Charlie Joiner, collection of the author

Green winged teal drake hunting decoy — head and chest detail

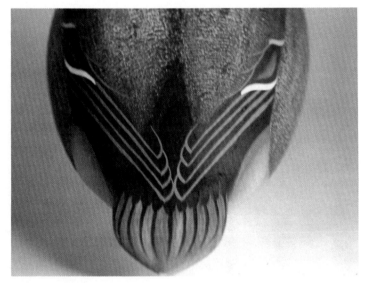

Green winged teal hunting decoy (drake) — primaries and tail area

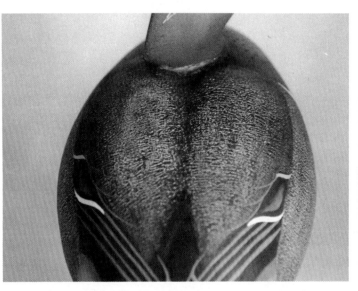

Green winged teal drake hunting decoy — back detail

Green winged teal drake hunting decoy — cheek — eye patch and bill detail

Green winged teal drake hunting decoy — side and tail area

Green winged teal hen hunting decoy — profile

Green winged teal hen hunting decoy — head, bill and sides detail

Green winged teal hen hunting decoy — head and chest detail

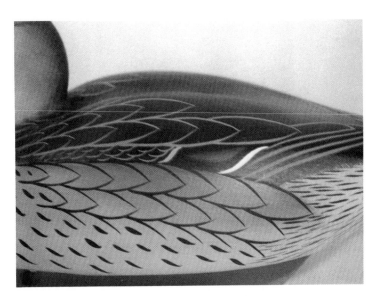

Green winged teal hen hunting decoy — side and rump detail

Green winged teal hen hunting decoy — side and rump detail

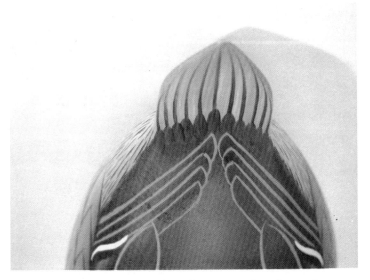

Green winged teal hen hunting decoy — primaries and tail detail

Blue winged teal hen hunting decoy copy of a Holly by Allen Purner

Blue winged teal hen decoy — head and bill detail

Blue winged teal hen decoy — side and tail area (hunting)

Blue winged teal hunting hen decoy head and bill detail

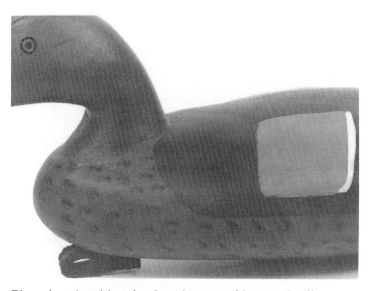

Blue winged teal hunting hen decoy — side area detail

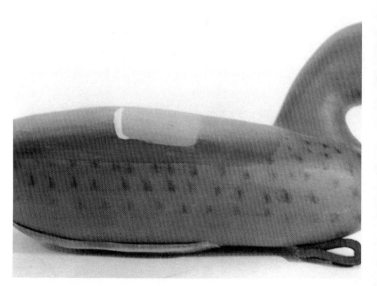

Blue winged teal hunting hen decoy side area

Bills

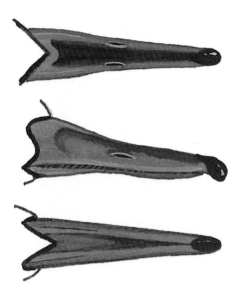

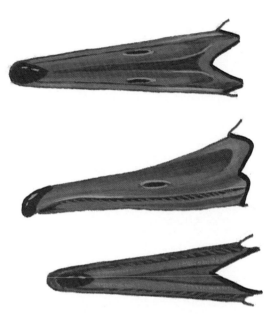

American Merganser—F—Black, White, Burnt Umber, Cadmium Red, and Cadmium Yellow

American Merganser—M—Black, White, Burnt Umber, Cadmium Red, and Cadmium Yellow

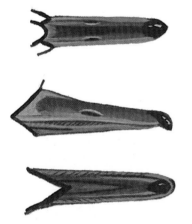

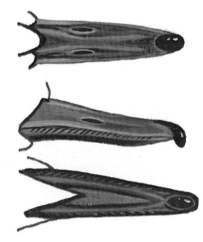

Hooded Merganser—F—Black, White, and Cadmium Yellow

Hooded Merganser—M—Black, White

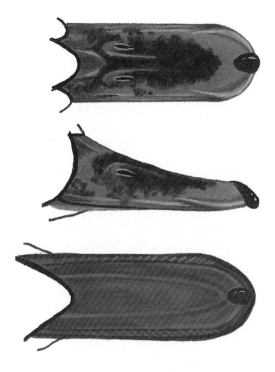

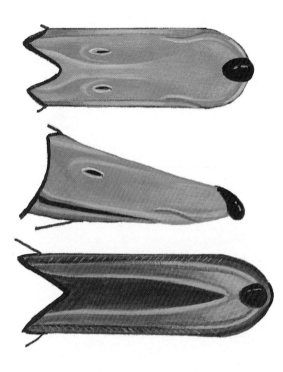

Mallard—F—Yellow Ochre, Cadmium Red, Cadmium
Yellow, Black, White, and Burnt Umber

Mallard—M—Black, White, and Yellow Ochre

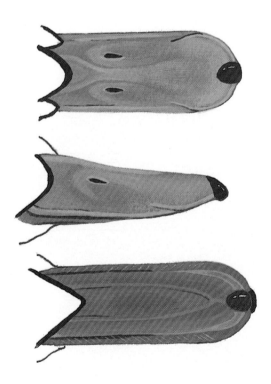

Black Duck—F & M—Black, White, and Yellow Ochre

Ruddy Duck—F & M—Black, White, and Ultra Marine
Blue

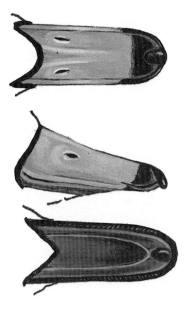

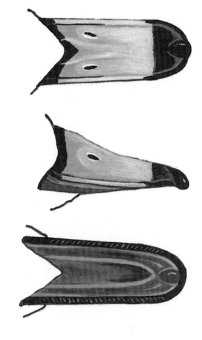

Baldplate—F—Black, White, Ultra Marine Blue, and Burnt Umber

Baldplate—M—Black, White, Ultra Marine Blue, and Burnt Umber

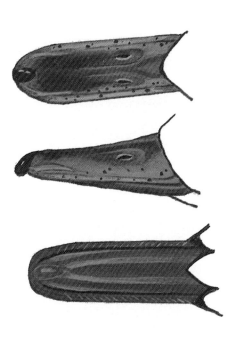

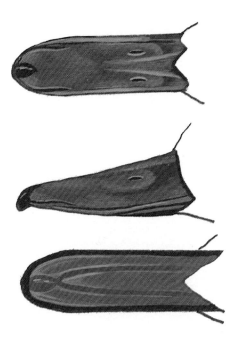

Gadwall—F—Black, White, Burnt Umber, Cadmium Red, and Cadmium Yellow Light

Gadwall—M—Black and White

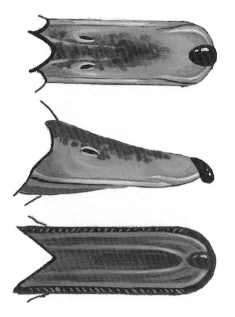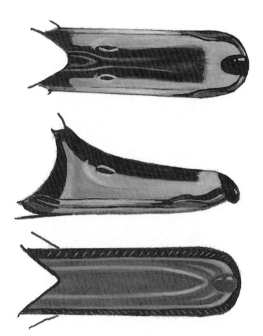

Pintail—F—Black, White, Ultra Marine Blue, and Burnt Umber

Pintail—M—Black, White, Ultra Marine Blue

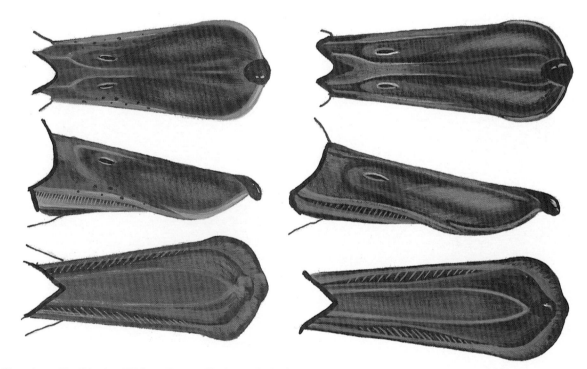

Shoveler—F—Black, White, Burnt Umber, Cadmium Yellow, and Cadmium Red

Shoveler—M—Black and White

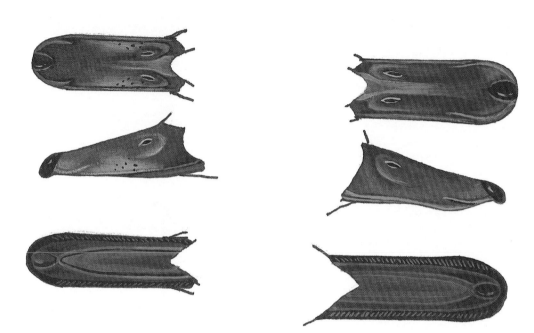

Blue winged teal—F—Black, White, and Burnt Umber

Blue winged teal—M—Black, White

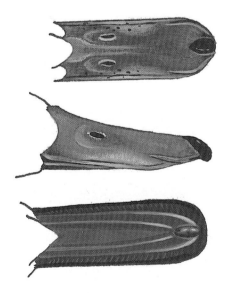

Cinnamon teal—M—Black, White

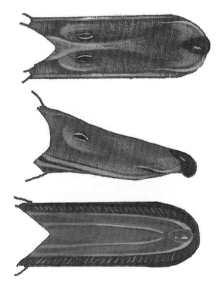

Cinnamon teal—F—Black, White, and Burnt Umber

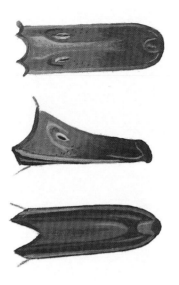

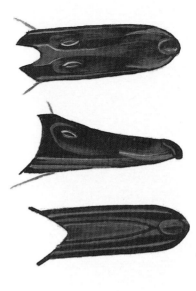

Green winged teal—F—Black, White, and Burnt Umber

Green winged teal—M—Black, White

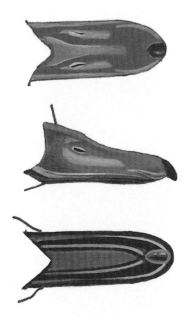

Wood Duck—F—Black, White, and Burnt Umber

Wood Duck—M—Black, White, Cadmium Red, and Yellow Ochre

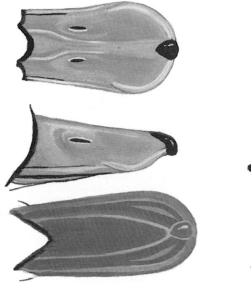
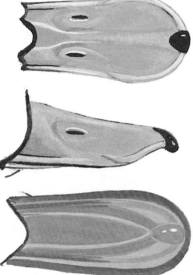

Lesser Scaup—F—Black, White, Ultra Marine Blue, and Burnt Umber

Lesser Scaup—M—Black, White, and Ultra Marine Blue

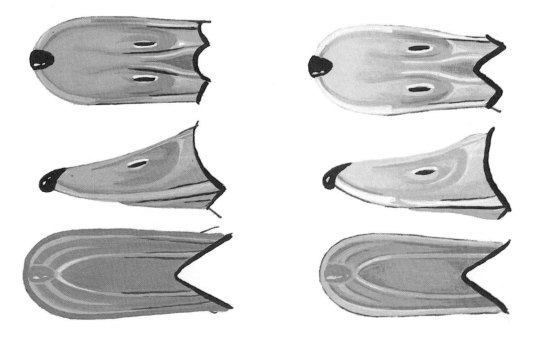

Greater Scaup—F—Black, White, Ultra Marine Blue, and Burnt Umber

Greater Scaup—M—Black, White, Ultra Marine

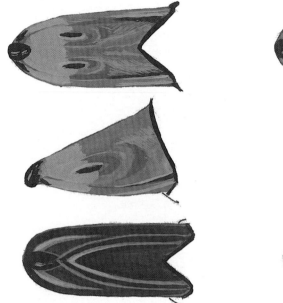

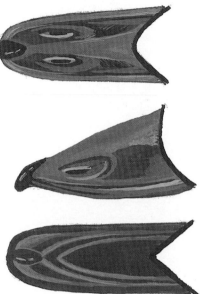

American Goldeneye—F—Black, White, Cadmium Yellow, and Cadmium Red

American Goldeneye—M—Black and White

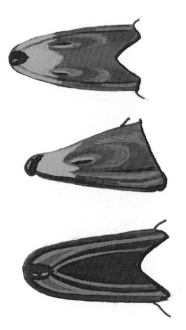

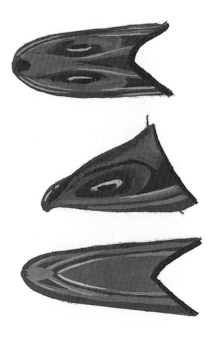

Barrows Goldeneye—F—Black, White, Cadmium Yellow, and Cadmium Red

Barrows Goldeneye—M—Black and White

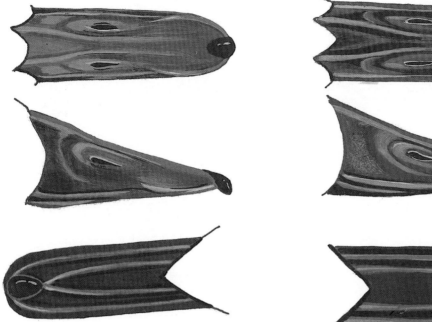

Canvasback—F—Black, and White

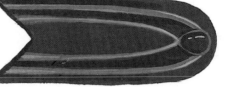

Canvasback—M—Black, White, and Burnt Umber

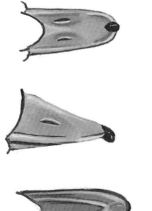

Bufflehead—M—Black, White, Burnt Umber, and Ultra Marine Blue

Bufflehead—F—Black, White, Burnt Umber, and Ultra Marine Blue

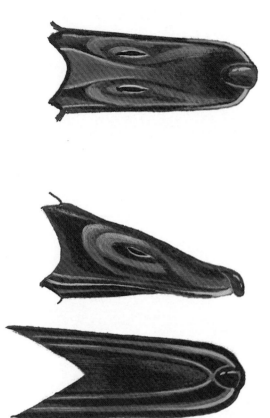

Canada Goose—F & M—Black, White

Brant—F & M—Black, White

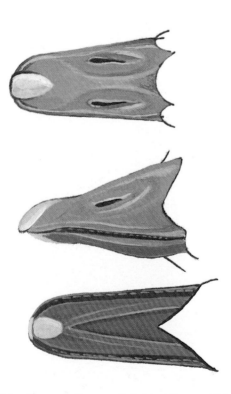

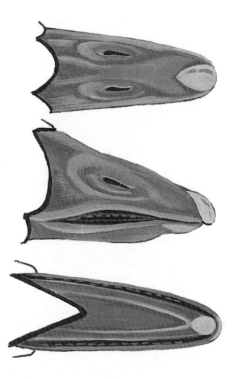

White Fronted Goose—F & M—Black, White Cadmium Red, and Cadmium Yellow

Snow/Blue Goose—F & M—Black, White, Cadmium Red, and Cadmium Yellow

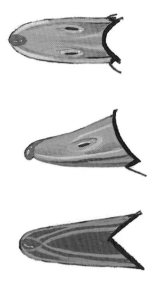 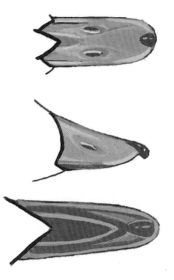

Harleqiun—F & M—Black, White, Burnt Umber, and
Ultra Marine Blue

Harleqiun—M—Black, White, Burnt Umber, and Ultra
Marine Blue

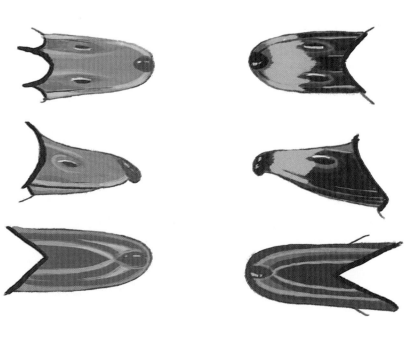

Old Squaw—F—Black, White, and Burnt Umber

Old Squaw—M—Black, White, Cadmium Red, and
Cadmium Yellow

Species: American Eider
Sex: Hen

PAINTING INSTRUCTIONS

Color list: *Black, White, Burnt umber.*
Body, Tail, and Wings: dark, dusky brown. Tips of feathers lighter.
Breast: paler brown, and the back: add a little white to it.
Hind Neck: dark, dusky brown.
Head, Crown: dark, dusky brown.
Cheek, Chin and Throat: pale gray, using black, white, and burnt umber. Finally barred and spotted with dusky—a darker hue of the same basic color.
Bill: blackish and streaked with yellow near the nostril.
Feet: olive to blackish.
Webs: dusky.

Species: American Eider
Sex: Drake

PAINTING INSTRUCTIONS

Color list: *Black, White, Burnt umber, Yellow ochre, Red, Hooker's green, Raw sienna.*
Tail and Coverts: black.
Rump: black. White patches at the flanks.
Breast, Belly, and Sides: black. Use black and ultra-marine blue.
Chest: white. Tinge with a pale, creamy brown. Raw sienna with a touch of burnt umber.
Wings and middle Coverts: white and dusky, along the forward edge of the wing.
Greater Coverts: black. In some cases: white tips. Sometimes mottled with a little grayish. Use black, white, and burnt umber.
Back and Scapulars: white, creamy white.
Tertials: white.
Outer Secondaries: black.
Inner Secondaries: white. Sickle shaped.
Primaries: black.
Cheek, Chin, Throat, and Neck: white.
Behind Head: sea green, using Hooker's green mixed with white. Extends forward under the black cap, almost to the bill.
Region around The Eye and Crown: irridescent glossy black. The crown is divided along the middle by a white streak, originating behind the head.
Bill: variable from gray to green. In spring it can be an orange-yellow.
Feet: yellow or green. Greenish with dusky webs.
Webs: use black, white, and burnt umber to make the dusky webs.
Nail: almost white, fused with bill.

Species: Eider
Sex: Hen

PAINTING INSTRUCTIONS

Color list: *Black, White, Burnt umber, Yellow ochre, Red, Hooker's green, Raw sienna, Burnt sienna.*
Tail: grayish brown, using black, white, and burnt umber.
Upper and Under Coverts: grayish brown, using black, white, and burnt umber.
Sides and Chest: feathers: brownish buff barred with blackish, and tipped with grayish buff.
Wings, lesser and middle Coverts: like the back; brownish with lots of grayish brown.
Greater Coverts: grayish brown tipped with white.
Breast and Belly: dusky brown.
Back and Scapular Feathers: brownish black broadly tipped, barred and mottled with rusty brown. Use burnt umber and burnt sienna for the rusty brown. Can also be mottled with buff. Raw sienna and white, touch of burnt umber.
Outer Secondaries: brownish-black, tipped with white.
Inner Secondaries and Tertials: rusty brown on the outer web, using burnt umber with a touch of burnt sienna. Brownish-black tipped with white. Brownish-black on the inner web. Lining brownish gray and white.
Primaries: black, brownish-black, using burnt umber and black.
Neck and Head: brown, finely streaked with black. Darker on the crown.
Bill: duller and greener than that of the male in winter.
Feet: grayish-yellow.
Webs: dusky, using black, white, burnt umber.
Nail: bone, yellow.

Species: Gadwall
Sex: Hen

PAINTING INSTRUCTIONS

Color list: *Black, White, Burnt umber, Raw sienna, Red, Yellow ochre.*
Tail, Tail Coverts: edged with white and raw sienna. Undercoat with burnt umber.
All Feathers: edge with white, mixed with raw sienna.
Primaries: burnt umber with a touch of white.
Head: white with raw sienna and a touch of burnt umber to make a dark buffy color. Eyeline is reinforced with burnt umber, touch of black. Also, all streaks and spots including crown and back of neck will be achieved with black and burnt umber to make a dark brown.
Bill: orangish, mottled with black and black spots.
Feet: yellow-orange.

Species: Harlequin Duck
Sex: Drake

PAINTING INSTRUCTIONS

Color list: *Black, White, Burnt umber, Burnt sienna, Yellow*

ochre, Payne's gray, Ultra-marine blue.
Tail: upper side: bluish-gray.   Under side: silvery-gray.
Rump: steely blue-black. Upper and under: blackish, mixed with ultra-marine blue.
Sides: Small white spot on the flank at the base of the tail. Reddish brown around ball and half way forward: burnt sienna with yellow ochre, blended into bluish gray.
Chest: blackish to gray, with a white band separating chest and breast area or chest and sides; banded with black.
Breast: slightly brownish color.
Belly: slaty brown to dusky.
Tertials: white banded with black.
Secondaries: ultra-marine blue.
Secondary Coverts: bluish, with Payne's gray and white and ultra-marine blue. Edged with white.
Primaries: burnt umber, touch of white. Lighter in the interior, darker on the edges. Purplish gloss.
Head: bluish gray with a white mask and white spots. Burnt sienna blended into the crown. White collar all the way around the head.
Bill: light grayish, using Payne's gray, white, with touch of burnt umber.
Feet: light gray.
Webs: blackish.
Toes: spotted with black.
Nail: yellowish.

Species: Harlequin Duck
Sex: Hen

PAINTING INSTRUCTIONS

Color list: *Black, White, Burnt umber, Raw umber, Thalo violet.*
Tail: dark purplish brown. Use a little violet with raw umber.
Upper and Under Coverts: olive brown.
Rump: brownish-black, using burnt umber and black.
Chest and Sides: paler brown. Add a little white to it; like the throat. Edge all the sides and back feathers lightly with white.
Wings: all coverts: dark brown, using burnt umber and raw umber, washed with olive brown.
Breast and Chest: grayish-white, mottled with grayish brown.
Belly: grayish-brown, using black, white, and burnt umber, mottled with a grayish-white.
Back and Scapulars: olive brown, using raw umber and a touch of white.
Tertials, Secondaries, and Primaries: dark gray, using black, white, and burnt umber. Wash some purple into it.
Neck and Head: dark, olive brown, using raw umber, with a touch of white. Darker on the crown. Large white spot under the eye and two smaller white spots. One in front of and above and the other behind the eye.
Chin and Throat: pale brown.
Bill: dusky, using black, white, and burnt umber.
Feet: light gray.

Species: Blue Goose
Sex: Drake and Hen

PAINTING INSTRUCTIONS

Color list: *Black, White, Burnt umber, Ultra-marine blue, Napthol crimson, Raw sienna.*
Tail and Rump: blackish.
Neck, Chest, Sides, and Back: use ultra-marine blue and burnt umber with a bit of white to create a dark, bluish-gray.
Feathers: edged with a darker hue of the same color, or almost black.
Tertial Feathers: have a black center and are edged with gray, and then an outer edge of white.
Primaries: black.
Head: white.
Bill and Feet: pinkish, using raw sienna, white, and napthol crimson.

Species: Snow Goose
Sex: Drake and Hen

PAINTING INSTRUCTIONS

Color list: *Black, White, Burnt umber, Raw sienna, Napthol crimson, Ultra-marine blue.*
Entire Bird: wash with a light tan, using burnt umber and white.
All Feathers: edged with white several times and wash with white several times until there is just a faint grayish color on the interior of the feather. Do a final wash with burnt umber, with just a touch of chalkiness.
Feather Edges: white with touch of ultra-marine blue for crispness.
Primaries: black. Use black and burnt umber or ultra-marine blue and burnt umber to make the black.
Forecheek and Forecrown: generally mottled with orangish tan, using raw sienna and white.
Bill: pinkish, using raw sienna, white, and napthol crimson.
Feet: pinkish.
Nail: whitish, brown, burnt umber grinning patch.

Species: Pied Billed Grebe
Sex: Drake and Hen

PAINTING INSTRUCTIONS

Color list: *Black, White, Burnt umber, Raw sienna.*
Entire Bird: undercoat of burnt umber with a touch of white.
All Side and Chest Feathers: edged in white, touch of raw sienna, wash with burnt umber.
Back and Crown: a little darker than the entire bird, washed with black.
Bill: white with a brown burnt umber band near the tip of the bill.
Feet: dark grayish brown, using black, white, burnt umber.

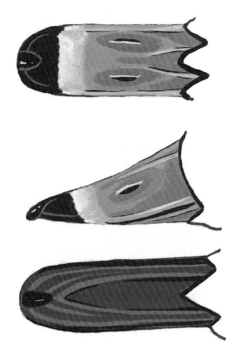

Red Head—F—Black, White, and Burnt Umber

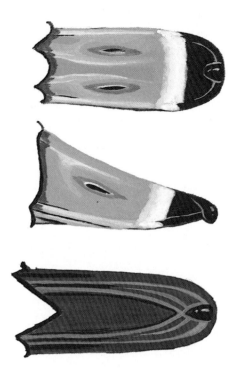

Red Head—M—Black, White, and Ultra Marine Blue

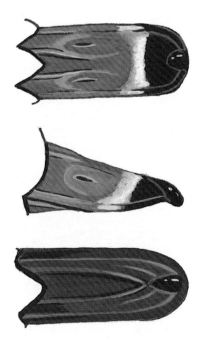

Ring Necked Duck—M—Black, White, Burnt Umber, and Ultra Marine Blue

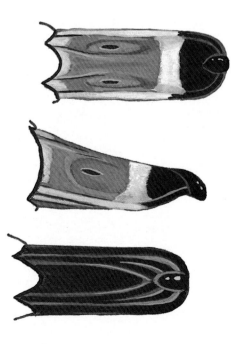

Ring Necked Duck—F—Black, White, and Burnt Umber

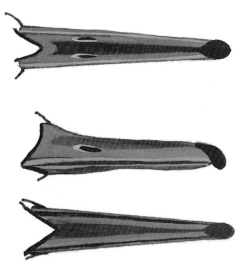 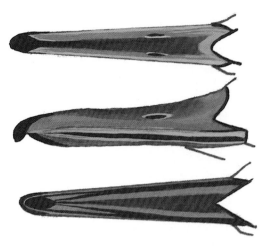

Red Breasted Merganser—F—Black, White, Cadmium Yellow, Cadmium Red, and Burnt Umber

Red Breasted Merganser—M—Black, White, Cadmium Yellow, Cadmium Red, and Burnt Umber

Species: American Scoter
Sex: drake

PAINTING INSTRUCTIONS

Color list: *Black, Burnt umber, Red, Yellow.*
Entire Bird: blackish-brown.
Bill: black. Exceptions: an orange protruberance at the base of the bill and runs then from the nostril to the head.

Species: Surf Scoter
Sex: Hen

PAINTING INSTRUCTIONS

Color list: *Black, White, Burnt umber, Yellow ochre.*
Body, Tail, and Wings: blackish brown. Mottled grayish, using black, white, and burnt umber. Between grayish and dusky.
Wing lining: dusky brown to silvery-brown.
Belly: dusky brown.
Neck and Head: dusky brown, using black, white, and burnt umber. The vague, whitish patch on the back of the head: whitish color being produced by using white with burnt umber added.
Crown, just below the eye: black.
Cheeks: two extra white patches. One over the ear and the other between the eye and the base of the bill.
Bill: blackish with a black patch at the base, surrounded by pale gray.
Feet: dull yellowish to dull brownish web.

Species: Surf Scoter
Sex: Drake

PAINTING INSTRUCTIONS

Color list: *Black, White, Burnt umber, Red, Yellow, Raw sienna, Napthol crimson.*
Body, Tail, and Wings and entire Back, Chest, Tail, and Wings: black.
Breast and Sides: brownish black. Use black and burnt umber.
Wing Line: brownish black and silvery-gray, using black, white, and burnt umber.
Belly: brownish black, mottled with lighter brown.
Lower Mandible: yellow toward the base and flesh color elsewhere. Use red, yellow, and raw sienna to make the flesh color.
Neck and Head: black on the male, except for a white patch on the forehead. A long train and patch of white in the nape.
The ridge and the region around the nostril: red.
Bill: square black patch on the side, near the base. Margin behind by red and above by orange.Use napthol crimson and yellow ochre to make the orange. In front and below a patch of white.
Feet: bright red on the outer side. Inner side: orange-red.
Webs: black.
Toes: marked with dusky.
Tip and Nail: pale yellow. Use yellow ochre and white.

Species: White Winged Scoter
Sex: Drake

PAINTING INSTRUCTIONS

Color list: *Black, White, Burnt umber, Red, Violet.*
Body and Tail: black with brownish tinge on the sides and chest.
Wings: black with tips and greater coverts and speculum white. Speck on the same secondaries.
Line: dusky brown to silvery brown.
Neck and Head: black. Use black mixed with burnt umber. A small white crescent spot behind and below the eye.
Bill edges of both Mandibles: black.
Sides of the upper Mandibles: red or purplish shading to orange near the base. Ridge is white. Crown of black—black knob at the base.
Lower Mandible: reddish-orange tip, white in center. Base black.
Feet: orange. Inner sides and outer sides: purplish-pink.
Webs: dusky to black.
Toes: irregularly marked with black.
Nail: large, fused, reddish-orange, often with narrow black lines on either side to bring back the knob.

Species: White Winged Scoter
Sex: Hen

PAINTING INSTRUCTIONS

Color list: *Black, White, Burnt umber, Red.*
Entire Body: blackish-brown.
Some Feathers, Sides, and Breast: edged with whitish.
Tail Coverts: blackish-brown.
Wings: blackish-brown with white secondaries.
Neck and Head: brownish-black, sometimes with two distinct lighter spots in the region of the ear and in front of the eye.
Bill: dull black, mixed with whitish in the upper mandible, sometimes a patch of deep pink on the sides.
Feet: light brownish-red.
Webs: blackish.

Species: Whistling Swan
Sex: Drake and Hen

PAINTING INSTRUCTIONS

Color list: *Black, White, Burnt umber, Yellow ochre.*
Entire Bird: undercoat with a light tan, using burnt umber and white.
All Feathers: edge with white several times—continue pulling into the feather and then wash with white several times. Final wash: burnt umber, very thin almost no pigment.
Bill: black with a yellow patch extending from the eye.
Feet: black.

Species: American Widgeon
Sex: Hen

PAINTING INSTRUCTIONS

Color list: *Black, White, Burnt umber, Burnt sienna, Payne's gray.*

Back, Chest, and Under Rump: undercoated with burnt umber.

Sides: undercoated with burnt umber, edged with white, and washed with a burnt sienna.

All Feathers: edged with white, touch of raw sienna.

All Spots: burnt umber with a touch of black.

Undercoat for the Head: raw sienna and white, with a touch of burnt umber to make a buffy color. Small streaks with burnt umber mixed with a touch of black.

Bill: Payne's gray and white.

Nail: black.

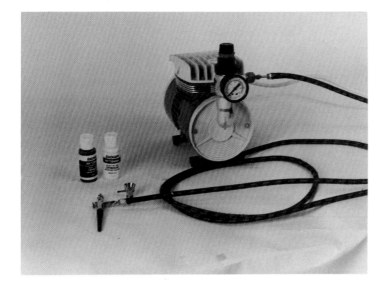

Typical air brush unit with compressor

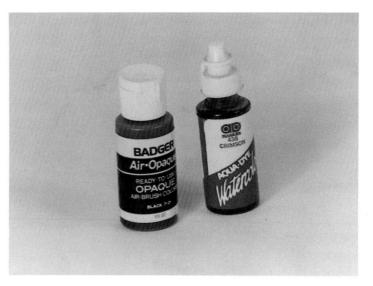

New badger opaque air brush paint

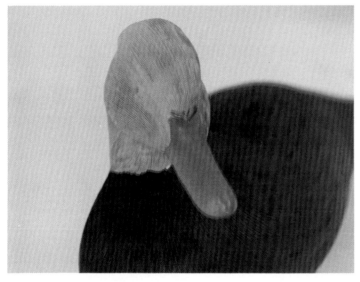

Teal hen under coated bill

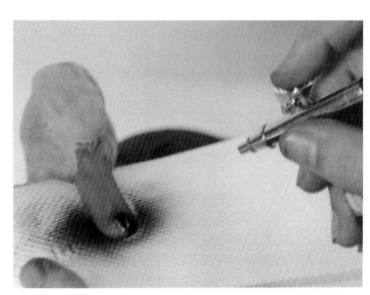

Air brush blending darker color on bill

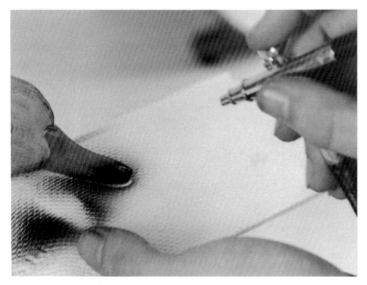

Air brush blending

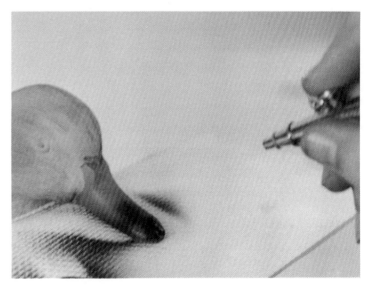

Air brush blending

184

Shading on back of head

Shading on forecheek and crown

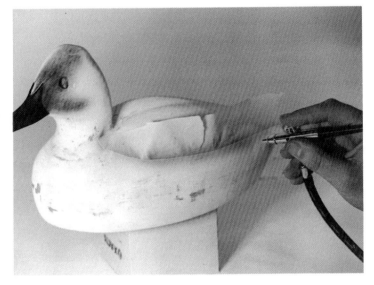

Shading on wing area

Shading on wing area

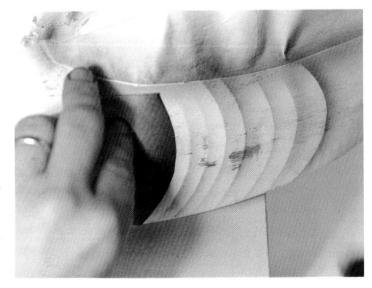

Stencil cut shading

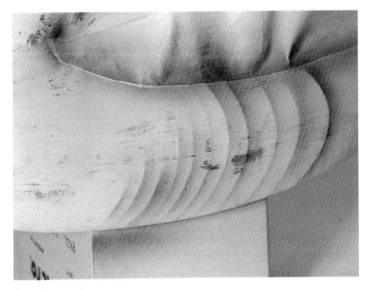

Stencil cut shading

Air Brush Technique

PREPARATION

A. Smooth birds (hunting)

1. Seal wood—any good wood sealer is okay if you use a coat of gesso over the sealer—if not then I would suggest a "soft sealer" e.g. cut shellac by at least one half—etc. as acrylic paint tends to lift off hard slick surfaces.

2. As a general rule I would suggest a coat or two of gesso on smooth birds sanding to 180 grit to smooth gesso.

3. Pencil or color chalk areas to be painted. Ideally a bird should be painted starting at tail and working forward.

B. Birds textured with Foredom tool

1. If wood is burned, use torch lightly and brush with vegetable brush then seal—Krylon or well cut shellac.

2. Coat with burnt umber to cover raw wood—begin painting.

C. Birds textured by burning

1. Clean texturing by lightly brushing
2. Spray lightly with Krylon, 1301 or 1303
3. White *wash* with acrylic paint
4. Begin to lay in base colors

How to Use the Air Brush

Screw airbrush into hose connection. Push color cup in place with a firm, screwing motion. Cup is held in position by a friction grip. Keep a uniform air pressure of 25 to 30 pounds.

Place some color in the color cup, hold the air brush in the manner of holding a pen, press with the forefinger upon the finger lever; this opens the air valve and produces a line or spray according to way air brush is set.

To increase the flow of color, pull the lever back (keeping the downward pressure), and at the same time draw air brush farther away from the work.

Do not let the lever fly forward with a click, but keep the downward pressure until lever comes forward, then release lever.

To Clean Air Brush

Air Brush must be cleaned thoroughly and at once after using. Most air brush trouble is caused by faulty cleaning.

When through using, fill color cup with clean water, blow plenty of clean water through the air brush, then while front lever is held back, place finger of left hand over opening of spray regulator so that air will bubble intermittently back into color cup. Repeat several times. Then unscrew connection nipple and insert in color cup, and pull back the finger lever, allowing the air to pass through the air brush; this will thoroughly dry the inside. Don't use hot water.

To Regulate Size of Line

Turn adjusting screw to the right (screw in) to increase the size of the line; to decrease, turn to the left (screw out).

To Regulate Quality of Spray

For average work (either line or spray) screw spray regulator all the way in; then back out 2 1/2-3 turns. Varying air pressure and consistency of color will determine the exact setting of spray regulator. Set spray regulator at position that is best for you. Do not switch spray regulator from one air brush to another as they are individually fitted.

To obtain the coursest spray screw spray regulator in. To obtain a fine spray unscrew spray regulator. Do not unscrew any further than necessary to obtain the quality of spray desired. After that, unscrewing spray regulator will weaken the suction and force the air into the color cup, and screwing in too far will stop the air. New style airbrushes must have spray regulator turned all the way down.

To Clean the Tip of the Air Bursh

Unscrew the handle. Loosen needle chuck by turning to left. Remove needle (if bent, straighten before removing), insert the cleaning reamer and turn from right to left only. Put a drop of oil on the reamer before inserting.

To Clean the Spray Regulator

Remove by unscrewing and clean with a cue stick. If your air brush throws specks, and the needle is not bent or the air brush injured in any way, it is quite likely that a bit of dust or dry color has lodged in spray regulator or on point of needle. Wipe point of needle when spray regulator is off by turning carefully between thumb and finger.

To Replace the Needle

Turn adjusting screw to the left, allowing front lever to go as far forward as possible; then insert needle, pressing it gently against the tip and tighten needle chuck; then turn adjusting screw one turn to the right, or until front lever no longer touches post.

To Replace the Tip

Remove needle and spray regulator as above. Fasten end of back reamer in hand chuck. Insert in air brush in same manner as needle. Push reamer firmly into old tip. Unscrew old tip by turning to the right, and remove from the air bursh. Do not attempt to repair a damaged tip, use a new one.

Start tip on threads of head by hand. Wax threads with beeswac. Now replace reamer in air bursh, inserting it firmly in inside of tip. Turn reamer and tip to the left until tight. Do not force tip as threads are very delicate. Use reamer (turning carefully) to remove burr on inside of tip. Replace needle and spray regulator as above.

Melt wax by heating with match. Then hold in vertical position with tip up until cool, so that wax will seal threads.

To Replace Head

To remove head assembly turn to left, using soft nosed pliers (use cloth, leather, or heavy paper in jaws to prevent marring.)

When replacing be sure teflon head seal is in place as threads must be waxed with beeswax before tightening. Unless threads are sealed a pulsating spray will develope.

To Clean Head

Remove head only after ordinary methods of cleaning have failed, and then only as a last resort. Soak in cold water. To use hot water will melt wax in tip threads and cause more trouble. Use round head (not point) of a small ordinary pin to scrape out loosened color. Be extra careful not to scratch inside of tip or to permit loosened color to pack in tip. Blow loose particles out with air. Use cleaning reamer to clean out tip only. Do not use any sharp instrument or poke inside of tip. Do not use a toothpick.

To Clean Color Cup

Remove cup from brush and screw color cup nut off. Clean hole in cup stem and bottom hole with sewing needle or straight pin. Soak in hot water and blow air into cup stem to remove dried color. Replace nut and replace in Airbrush.

To Replace Valve Washers

The rubber washer will sometimes become gummy from oil, and expand, causing the air valve to clog up. This is remedied by a new washer. To replace, remove the screw at bottom of valve; the spring and plunger will then drop out. With a pin remove the rubber washer and insert a new one, forcing it into place with a match, then replace plunger, spring and valve nut.

Don't

Don't use hot water for cleaning air brush.

Don't take the air brush apart at your first trouble. See if your air pressure is right; try running clean water through; see if your spray regulator is adjusted right; see if your needle is set for the line you want.

Don't bend the point of the needle.

Don't insert anything in spray regulator when it is on the air brush.

Don't enlarge opening in spray regulator.

Don't use the reamer except in extreme cases, and do not press to hard when turning it.

Don't insert anything in tip, or pinch or batter it in any way.

Don't let your colors be exposed to dirt and lint.

Don't use any colors that are not finely ground.

Don't let others handle your brush, and loan it as little as possible.

Don't fail to keep spray regulator free from dried color.

Don't spoil thread on spray regulator by starting in wrong and then forcing it.

Don't snap front lever.

Proficient use of the Air Brush is gained only after you thoroughly know the major parts of the Air Brush and how they operate.

The Mechanical Controls

The trigger button is the square, chrome-plated button on top of the Air Brush. This is a single-action control in that it controls only the flow of air. Some air brushes have a double-action trigger button which controls both the flow of air and the amount of fluid being sprayed.

The small, knurled screw just below the trigger button limits the movement of the trigger button and the flow of air. This screw should be turned down (to the left) as far as it will go. Only when a spatter or stipple effect is desired should the trigger button screw be raised to the position just below the extended trigger button. Experimenting with the screw in different positions will provide a variety of lighter to heavier spatter patterns. The color droplets will increase in size as the screw is turned higher, cutting down the flow of air.

The air intake is located on the bottom of the Air Brush in line with the slanted trigger button. Screw the small end of the air hose to the air intake and tighten with a wrench until snug.

The fluid control is located under the front end of the Air Brush and protrudes into the nozzle. The knurled portion of the fluid central opens or closes the flow of fluid. Turning the control clockwise opens it wider, counter-clockwise closes it.

The color bottle assembly has a friction connection which is inserted into the opening at the bottom of the fluid central (see photograph), and is fastened with a firm push-and-twist motion. Look for a small vent hole in the lid of the bottle assembly. This hole should be kept open and free of fluid because if it becomes clogged, the flow of air into the bottle is blocked, preventing the flow of color upward into the fluid control.

The air needed to operate the Air Brush can be obtained from pressure cans such as Binks Wren Paks, or individual air compressors such as portable or larger tank-mounted compressors. The air pressure should be about 38 pounds per square inch when the Air Brush is not spraying; it should drop to about 30 per per square inch when in operation. Be sure that all hose connections are tight to prevent leakage.

Use of the Air Brush

The colors to be sprayed, or air brushed, should be thoroughly mixed and free of lumps or pigment or other impurities. It is wise to strain the fluids through a piece of nylon hose as you pour them into the color bottles. Your colors and paints may have to be thinned down to permit them to flow through the Air Brush.

The Air Brush should be held much like a pencil, with the index finger operating the trigger button. The air hose should pass below the thumb and over the wrist to keep it out of the way.

Air brushing should be done in short strokes, or bursts. Depress and release the trigger button with each stroke. This will quickly become a habit.

Now you are ready to start. Choose a dark color to spray so you can see what is occuring. First, turn the fluid control counter-clockwise to close it. Hold the air brush about a half-inch from the paper and depress the trigger button. Slowly open the fluid control until a wisp of color appears. It will make a small dot or, as you slowly move your hand, a small, fine line. As you open the fluid control wider, move the Air Brush back away from the paper and a wider line will be sprayed. Continue experimenting in this manner to learn what can be done with the Air Brush. The use of stencils or straight edges can quickly give varied and pleasing effects. Highlights and depth are created by air brushing some areas more lightly, or by letting the background colors show through. Stencils can be used for spraying many shapes.

OPERATION
Thinning Fluids

Fluids that may be sprayed with the Air Brush range from light, or water type consistency to heavy, or enamel type consistency It is most desirable that the fluid be of a viscosity that is sparyable, provides adequate coverage and yet will not run or sag. To achieve this, reduction, or thinning of the fluid may be necessary. When and how to correctly reduce or thin fluids is a matter of judgement and common sense.

Straining Fluids

Since the fluid orifices in the Air Brush are extremely small, it is essential that the fluid to be sprayed be free of foreign particles. It is recommended that fluids be strained through a piece of nylon stocking or similar mesh cloth before use.

Housekeeping

Ninety-five percent of breakdowns in the operation of an Air Brush are directly due to not keeping the Air Brush clean at all times, especially after each use. When using fast drying fluids, such as lacquers, underglazes, etc. which will set up in five to ten minutes, it may be necessary to clean or immerse the fluid control end of the Air Brush in compatible solvent during intermittent use.

Vermiculations

Many male ducks and some female ducks have vermiculations on some of their feathers. Vermiculations are striations of color, thin lines that appear to be random because of the way feathers lie but actually are fairly regular. They are generally on the sides and back of a bird, and sometimes extend through the tertials or down the rump or into the hindmost part of the chest.

Vermiculations are usually black, white, brown or brownish-gray on a white base, but differ with every bird. Study the species to find the exact color of the vermiculations and the feathers they are on, as well as the area of vermiculations.

If you are going to carve a species that has vermiculations in life, you should include them in your carving. Find a method you can do well. I've seen a number of really fine, well-carved birds that have poorly done vermiculations. It's always better to do simple vermiculations well than to attempt a complicated version and do it badly.

Here are several methods of producing vermiculations. The first few are simple ones that give the broad illusion of vermiculations rather than a totally accurate version. But if you're doing a fairly simple carving these simple vermiculations look just fine. All the methods are possible to do, even for the novice carver, if time is taken to practice. Experiment with the following methods on a board until you find vermiculations that you are able to do well. Then work on the carving.

On a smooth surface, undercoat the area to be vermiculated with very thick gesso or a mixture of gesso and modeling paste. If the base color of the bird isn't white, tint the gesso to the correct color.

With an ordinary pocket comb put swirls through the gesso and allow it to air dry. Do not dry with a hair dryer because if modeling paste dries too fast it cracks; if you hold the hairdryer too close to gesso, the ridges blow out.

Mix the color for the vermiculations to a heavy-cream consistency and paint it over the combed area. Let the paint dry, then lightly sand with 120 grit sandpaper to knock off the high spots you made with the comb. Apply a toning wash of ultra-thin burnt umber to tone down the starkness of the base color.

A variation of this method is to make swirls in the gesso with a stiff bristle brush.

On a smooth surface, undercoat areas to be vermiculated with gesso, just as you did in the previous method. After it is dry, brush on a thick coat of the base color in acrylic artist paint. While this is still wet, stipple it with a stiff brush so it looks stuccoed. Allow it to dry, then paint on the vermiculation color in a heavy-cream consistency. Let the paint dry, lightly sand, and apply the toning wash of ultra-thin burnt umber.

On a smooth or textured surface (it is not as good on a textured surface) paint the base color on the area to be vermiculated. Use a thicker consistency than your usual base wash. Mix matte medium (a varnish that is flat) with a tiny bit of color for the vermiculations and brush it on the base color. With a wash brush or a round red sable brush, depending on the look you want, pat and push the medium to create ripples and streaks. Let it air dry (a hairdryer will blow away the little waves you've created). Finish with an ultra-thin burnt umber toning wash.

Now the procedures become more realistic. On a smooth or textured surface, paint the base color.

Decide what color the vermiculations are. Let's say they'll be white and black. Put some thinned white paint on you palette and build up the paint in a trimmed #8 round red sable brush. Very lightly apply the paint, holding the slightly cupped brush at a 90° angle to the surface. Leave little flecks of color in a lenghtwise row across the area. Turn the bird around in your hand, and paint another row next to the first one; turn again and paint a third row; and so on. This creates a waviness rather than rows of arced feathers. Let the white paint dry. Then build up some black paint in the cleaned brush and paint on rows of black in the same way, overlapping the two colors slightly. Go back to white, then black, and so on. The more times you do this, the more the flecks of color will meld together to simulate vermiculations. Take your time; the job looks better if you don't rush. Finish with the ultra-thin burnt umber toning wash.

On a smooth or textured surface (textured is best) us a permanent felt-tip pen. The Finliner Pilot Pen by Sc-uf or a Sharpee Pen that has a broader point do well. Both come in black; and in brown. Therefore you can use this method only if your vermiculations are those colors.

Undercoat the area to be vermiculated with the base paint. Draw the layout of the feathers that will be vermiculated. With the pen, draw squiggly lines starting at the innermost point of a feather and working outward until that feather is done. Then go on to the next. Do not try to do each feather exactly the same, because the effect will be too stiff. This is going to take a lot of time to do right. A problem with this method is if the bird's vermiculations appear to be gray. If so, wash over your black vermiculations with a white wash to soften them. This makes the surface look chalky, therefore you must finish with a burnt umber wash.

Another method is done in the same way, but here the vermiculations are done with a quill pen, using your choice of points by Speedball. The advantage of this method is that you can use any color of acrylic paint you need. Use a very thin paint consistency, like ink.

This procedure can be done on a smooth or textured surface, but it looks the best on the latter. This method is the most sophisticated because it enables you to highlight one area and darken another; you can't do this with any of the previous methods.

Undercoat different areas in different colors, or different hues of the same color, according to the color of the actual bird. Perhaps you will undercoat one area with gray and another area with white. Draw the outlines of the feathers. Paint squiggly lines for the vermiculation with a 0 round red sable brush or a #2 or #4 script brush, using any color acrylic paint you need in a fairly thin consistency. Let's say that on the gray undercoat you will vermiculate with black, then on the white undercoat you'll vermiculate with gray. This method won't look very good in the beginning, but keep doing it until the colors meld and really look like the actual bird colors. Finish with the toning wash of ultra-thin burnt umber.

After all the vermiculations are done (by whatever method), highlight the edges of the feathers with white paint in a heavy-cream consistency. Don't apply it heavily. Pull the flat edge of the brush into a feather, following the lines you drew, and then lift the brush out, leaving a slightly jagged edge on the interior of the feather. In the first few methods, if you choose to highlight the feathers, draw these lines with chalk and then edge the feathers.

When you are vermiculating your bird, do the vermiculations at about the same time you do the feather edgings. Do not try to precisely copy the vermiculations on one side of the bird on the other side, because the effect will be too stiff. If you happen to mess up the vermiculations cover then with a couple of base washes of paint and start again. But if this happens too often, you'll fill in all the texturing and will have to sand down the bird and start again.

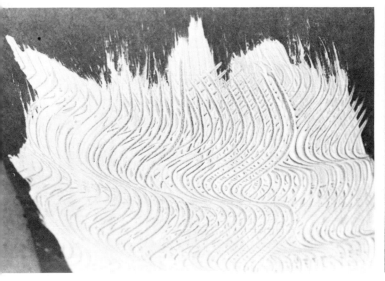

Example combed gesso

Example stippled gesso and modeling paste

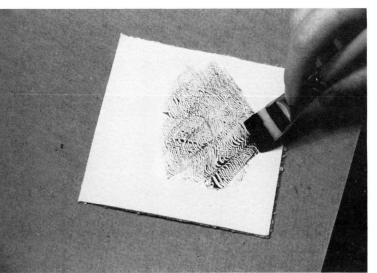

Example overbrushing combed area

Example swirled with stiff brush

Example of alternate black and white stippling with trimmed #8 round red sable on sides of green winged teal drake

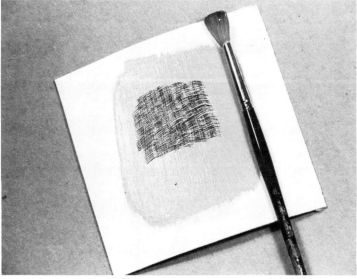

Example of left on palette board

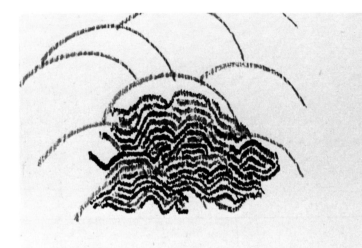

Finer vermiculation with pen

Broad vermiculation using quill pen

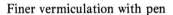
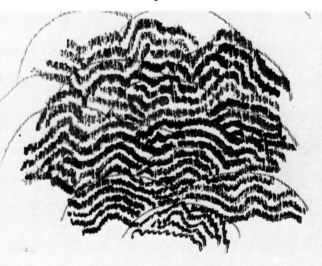

More vericulation practice with quill pen

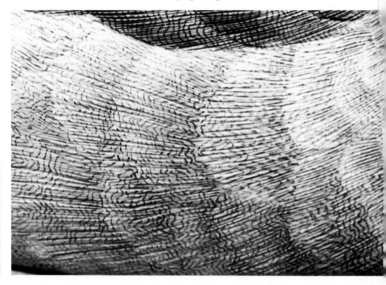

Example of vermiculations done with pilot pen on textured surface and feather edged highlighted to create a layered effect.

Example of practice pad layout for vermiculating with pilot pen

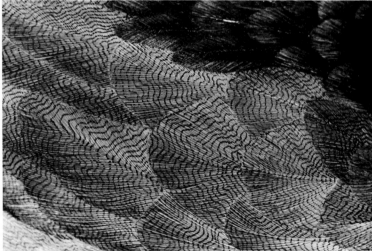

Example of vermiculations done with pilot pen on textured surface of individually carved feathers which create their own depth; however shading should be used to further create highlights and shadow.

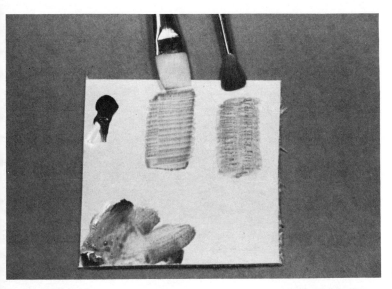

Creating ripples and streaks in matte medium

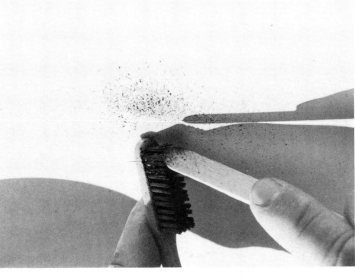

Example of vermiculation by spritzing with tooth brush; top left — picking up color (wet) on toothbrush; top right — example of using craft stick to run across brush to spritz; bottom left — example of same but end of stroke; bottom right — example of spritzed area excellant for smooth bodied birds — hunting decoys etc.

Unusual Studies

Snow Goose

Snow Goose

Snow Goose

White fronted goose

Three white fronted geese

White fronted goose

Whistling swan

Whistling swan

Whistling swan — head detail

Whistling swan — family

Canada goose — pair

Red breasted geese — pair

American goldeneye drake

American goldeneye drake

American goldeneye hen

American goldeneye pair

American goldeneye pair

American goldeneye drake

American goldeneye drake

Barrows Goldeneye

Barrows Goldeneye

Canvasback drake — sleeper position

Canvasback drake

Canvasback drake

Canvasback hen

Hooded merganser drake

Hooded merganser hen

Hooded merganser hen

Hooded merganser drake

Hooded merganser drake

Hooded merganser hen

Cinnamon teal — pair

Cinnamon teal — pair

Cinnamon teal — pair

Blue winged teal — pair

Blue winged teal — pair

Blue winged teal hen

Blue winged teal drake

204

American eider drake — head detail

American eider drake — bill detail

American eider drake — chest detail

American eider drake — side detail

American Eider Hen — bill detail

American eider hen — tail detail

American eider hen — side detail

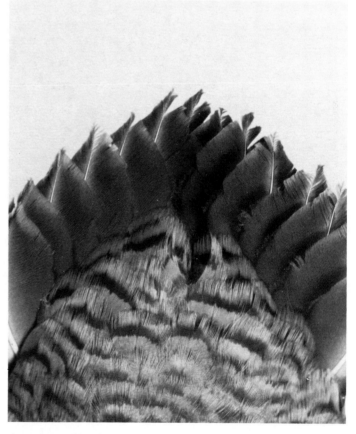

American eider hen — rump detail

American Eider pair

Fulvous tree or whistling ducks

Mandarin drake

Mandarin drake

207

Red head drake

Red head hen

Red head pair

Red head

Red Head — pair

Red head — pair

Red head — pair

Red head hen

Red head hen

Pintail drake

Pintail drake

Pintail drake

Pintail pair

Green winged teal pair

Green winged teal drake

Ring necked duck drake

Ringed necked duck drake

Scaup drake

Scaup drake

Scaup drake

Scaup drake

Ruddy duck — pair

Ruddy duck drake

Ruddy duck hen

Ruddy duck drake

Ruddy duck drake

Ruddy duck drakes

Ruddy duck drake

Ruddy duck hen

Ruddy duck pair

215

Shoveler hen

Shoveler drake

Shoveler drake preening

Shoveler pair

Shoveler drake

Mallard hen with young

Mallard pair in flight

Mallard — two drakes — one hen

Widgeon hen

Widgeon drake

Widgeon drake

218

Widgeon drake

Widgeon drake

Widgeon drake

Widgeon pair

Widgeon hen

Widgeon — pair

Wood duck — pair

Wood duck hen

Wood duck drake

Wood duck hen

Gadwall pair

Gadwall drake

Gadwall drake

Gadwall drake

Source Books

A Field Guide to the Birds Eastern Land and Water Birds. *Roger Tory Peterson.* Houghton Mifflin Company

A Field Guide in Color to Birds. *Dr. Walter Ceony.* Octopus Books, Limited

A Field Guide to the Nests, Eggs and Nestlings of British and European Birds. *Colin Harrison.* Demeter Press, Incorporated

A Guide to Field Indentification Birds of North America. *Chandler S. Robbins, Bentel Brown & Herbert Zim.* Wester Publishing Company, Incorporated

A Sketchbook of Birds. *Charles Tunnicliffe.* Holt, Rinehart & Winston

American Water & Game Birds. *Austin L. Rand.* E. P. Dutton & Company, Incorporated

Anatomy of a Waterfowl, for carvers and painters. *Charles W. Frank, Jr.* Pelican Publishing Company

Birds, Birds, Birds, Birds, Birds, Birds. The Hamlyn Publishing Group, Limited

Birds of Prey. *Gareth Parry & Rory Putman.* Simon & Schuster

Chip Chats. National Wood Carvers Association

Cranes of the World. *Lawrence Waltinshaw.* Winchester Press

Ducks Unlimited. Ducks Unlimited, Incorporated

Game Bird Carving. *Bruce Burk.* Winchester Press

Lambert's Birds of Shore and Estuary. *Test by Alan Mitchell, Paintings by Terence Lambers.* Charles Scribner's Sons

North American Decoys. Hillcrest Publications, Incorporated

Song Birds. *Introduction by D. H. S. Ridson.* Crescent Books

The Art of Audubon the complete Birds and Mammals. *John James Audubon* with *Introduction by Roger Tory Peterson.* Times Books

The Living World of Audubon. *Roland C. Clement.* The Ridge Press, Incorporated

Top Flight Field Guide. *John A. Ruthven* and *William Zimmerman.* Moebius Printing Company

The Audubon Society Encyclopedia of North American Birds. *John K. Terres.* Alfred A. Knopf, Incorporated

Ward Foundation News. The Ward Foundation

Waterfowl Carving, Blue Ribbon Techniques. *William Veasey* with *Cary Schuler Hull.* Schiffer Publishers

Waterfowl Ducks, Geese and Swans of the World. *Frank S. Todd.* Sea World, Incorporated

Waterfowl Studies. *Bruce Burk.* Winchester Press.

Wildlife in Wood. *Richard LeMaster.* Richard LeMaster

Index

A

acrylic paint, 14, 15, 16, 186
air brush, 184, 185, 186
Alderson, Jack, 41, 92, 99, 104, 109, 157
alkyd paint, 13
American eider drake, 178, 205, 207
American eider hen, 178, 206, 207
American goldeneye drake, 117, 198, 199
    bill, 174
    color chart, 118
American goldeneye hen, 114, 117, 199
    bill, 174
    color chart, 113
    decoy, 112, 114
American merganser drake, 131
    bill, 167
    color chart, 132
    decoy, 131
American merganser hen, 131
    bill, 167
    color chart, 133
American scoter drake, 182
American widgeon drake, 87
    color chart, 88
American widgeon hen, 183
Arnold, Eldridge, 9
Atlantic brant decoy, 19, 20

B

baldpate drake–bill, 169
baldpate hen–bill, 169
Barrow's goldeneye, 200
Barrow's goldeneye drake, 115
    bill, 174
    color chart, 116
Barrow's goldeneye hen, 112
    bill, 174
    color chart, 113
Bartrug, Knute R., 9
belly of hair, 15
bills, 167–183
Binney and Smith, Liquitex, 16
Birch, New England, 13
Birch, Tom, 17, 38, 44
Black duck, 33
    color chart, 31
    decoy, 30, 32
Black duck drake, 30
    bill, 168
Black duck hen, 30
    bill, 168
Blue goose (see snow goose), 26
Blue goose drake, 179
Blue goose hen, 179
Blue winged teal decoy, 64
Blue winged teal drake, 67, 69, 204
    bill, 171
    color chart, 68
    decoy, 70

Blue winged teal hen, 64, 66, 67, 204
    bill, 171
    color chart, 65
    hunting decoy, 166
Brant, 17, 18
    color chart, 18
    decoy, 17
    drake, 17
        bill, 176
    hen, 17
        bill, 176
bristle, 15
brush, camel hair, 14
brush, cleaning, 13
brush, goat hair, 14
brush, ox hair, 14
brush parts, 16
brush, pony hair, 14
brush, red sable, 14
brush, squirrel hair, 14
brush, synthetic, 14
brushes, 13–16
Bufflehead drake, 96, 98
Bufflehead drake bill, 175
    color chart, 97
Bufflehead hen, 99, 101
    bill, 175
    color chart, 100
    decoy, 99
butt of hair, 15

C

Calvert, Jan, 163
camel hair brush, 14
Canada goose, 21, 181, 197
    color chart, 23
Canada goose drake, 22
    bill, 176
Canada goose hen, 22
    bill, 176
Canvasback drake, 102, 105, 106, 201
    bill, 175
    color chart, 103
    decoy, 104
Canvasback hen, 107, 201
    bill, 175
    color chart, 108
    decoy, 109
Canvasback hunting decoy, 162, 163
Carney, Armand, 9
Chinese White, 11
Christoflich, Anthony, 131
Cinnamon teal, 203
Cinnamon teal drake, 71, 74, 76
    bill, 171
    color chart, 75
Cinnamon teal hen, 71, 73
    bill, 171

Cinnamon teal hen, continued
    color chart, 72
Common loon, 110
    color chart, 111
    decoy, 110
Constable (John), 11
Cygnet, 29

D

Dohl, Claude, 161

E

easel painting, 14
Eider (see American eider)
Eider hen, 178
emulsion paint, 16
Ewell, Ned, 9
exotic hen, 54

F

ferrule, 13, 16
Field, George, 11
Fitrovia, 11
Floyd, John, 162
Foredom tool, 186
Furness, Nan, 9

G

Gadwall, 34
Gadwall drake, 34, 36, 40, 221
    bill, 169
    color chart, 35
    decoy, 37
Gadwall hen, 34, 39, 178, 221
    bill, 169
    decoy, 38
gesso, 186
Goldeneye (see American goldeneye,
    Barrow's goldeneye)
Greater scaup drake, 155, 157
    bill, 173
    color chart, 156
Greater scaup hen, 157, 158
    bill, 173
    color chart, 159
Grebe (see Pied billed grebe)
Green winged teal drake, 81, 82, 84, 85, 86, 211
    bill, 172
    decoy, 81, 83
    hunting decoy, 164, 165
Green winged teal hen, 78, 79, 86, 211
    bill, 172
    decoy, 77, 80
goat hair brush, 14
goose (see Blue goose, Snow goose,
    White fronted goose)

goose, 22, 24
goose, Blue, 26
goose, Richardson, 26
goose, White fronted, 25
Grumbacher, 16
Grumbacher brush, 15
gum arabic solution, 15

H

hair, 15
Ham, E.J., 7
handles, brush, 13, 16
Harlequin duck drake, 178
    bill, 177
Harlequin duck hen, 179
    bill, 177
Hazzard, William, 10
Hollestelle, Cliff, 10
Holly, 166
Hooded merganser drake, 119, 121, 122, 202
    bill, 167
       color chart, 120
       decoy, 121, 122
Hooded merganser hen, 119, 123, 125, 202
    bill, 167
       color chart, 124
Hopkins, Hal, 55
Hunt (Speedball), 16
hunting decoys, 160–166

J

Joiner, Charlie, 164

K

Kershaw County Vocational Center, Camden, South Carolina, 7
Kline, Joe, 161
Kolinsky, 14
Kolinsky, North Asian, 13
Krylon, 186
Kurman, Sina "Pat", 30, 46, 77, 145

L

lacquering, 14
Lesser scaup decoy, 158
Lesser scaup drake, 155
    bill, 173
       decoy, 157
Lesser scaup hen, 158
    bill, 173
Liquitex (Binney and Smith), 16
Loon, common, 110

M

Mace, Penny, 29, 51, 64
Mallard drake, 44, 47, 48, 49, 50, 217
    bill, 168
       color chart, 45
       decoy, 44, 48
Mallard hen, 41, 46, 50, 217
    bill, 168
       color chart, 42
       decoy, 43, 46
Merganser (see American merganser, Hooded Merganser, Red breasted merganser)
Miller, Penny, 10
mink, 13
Moffett, Ralph, 86

N

New England birch, 13
Newton, Henry, 11

North Asian Kolinsky, 13
nylon filaments, 15

O

oil paint, 13, 15
Old squaw, 139
Old squaw drake, 139, 141, 177
    color chart, 142
Old squaw hen, 139
    bill, 177
    color chart, 140
ox hair brush, 14

P

paint, acrylic, 14, 16
    alkyd, 13
    emulsion, 16
    oil, 13
    tempera, 14
    water color, 14
painting, easel, 14
Pied billed grebe drake, 179
Pied billed grebe hen, 179
pilot pen, 192
Pintail, 54
Pintail drake, 56, 57, 58, 210
    bill, 170
    color chart, 59
    decoy, 55
Pintail hen, 210
    bill, 170
    color chart, 52
    decoy, 51, 53
Pintail hunting decoy, 161
pony hair brush, 14
Purner, Allen, 166

Q

quill pen, 192

R

Red breasted goose, 197
Red breasted merganser, 126
Red breasted merganser drake, 126, 128
    bill, 181
    color chart, 127
Red breasted merganser hen, 129
    bill, 181
    color chart, 130
Red head drake, 143, 145, 146, 208, 209
    bill, 180
    color chart, 144
    decoy, 143
Red head hen, 147, 149, 208, 209
    bill, 180
    color chart, 148
red sable brush, 14, 15
resin, 16
Richardson goose, 26
Ring necked duck, 136
Ring necked duck drake, 134, 212
    bill, 180
    color chart, 135
Ring necked duck hen, 137, 138
    bill, 180
Ring necked duck hunting decoy, 160
Ruddy duck drake, 150, 152, 214, 215
    bill, 168
    color chart, 151
Ruddy duck hen, 153, 154, 214, 215
    bill, 168

S

sable brush, 13

Sasser, Dr. Marshall, 160
Scaup (see Greater scaup, Lesser scaup)
Scaup drake, 213
Scoter (see American scoter, Surf scoter, White winged scoter)
series 7 sable brush, 13
shading, 185
shellac, 186
Shoveler drake, 62, 216
    bill, 170
    color chart, 63
Shoveler hen, 60, 216
    bill, 170
    color chart, 61
Simmons, Robert, brush, 15
Snow goose (see Blue goose), 194
Snow goose drake, 179
Snow or Blue goose drake–bill, 176
Snow goose hen, 179
Snow or Blue goose hen–bill, 176
Speedball, Hunt, 16
Sprankle, Jim, 10
squirrel hair brush, 14
stencil cut shading, 185
Surf scoter drake, 182
Surf scoter hen, 182
Sutton, Robert, 10
Swan, 27, 28
    decoy, 29
Swan, Whistling, 182, 196
synthetic hair brush, 15

T

Teal (see Blue winged teal, Green winged teal)
Teal hen, 184
tempera paint, 14

V

Veasey Studios, 15
vermiculations, 189–193

W

Ward brothers decoy, copy, 163
watercolor paint, 14, 15
weasel, 14
Whistling swan, 182, 196
White fronted goose, 25, 195
White fronted goose drake–bill, 176
White fronted goose hen–bill, 176
White winged scoter drake, 182
White winged scoter hen, 182
Widgeon (see American widgeon)
Widgeon drake, 218, 219
Widgeon hen, 218, 219
Winsor, William, 11
Winsor & Newton, 11, 13, 16
Wood duck drake, 92, 94, 95, 220
    bill, 172
    color chart, 93
    decoy, 92
Wood duck hen, 89, 91, 220
    bill, 172
    color chart, 90
Woolard, Gil, 7
Wooster, Joe, 10

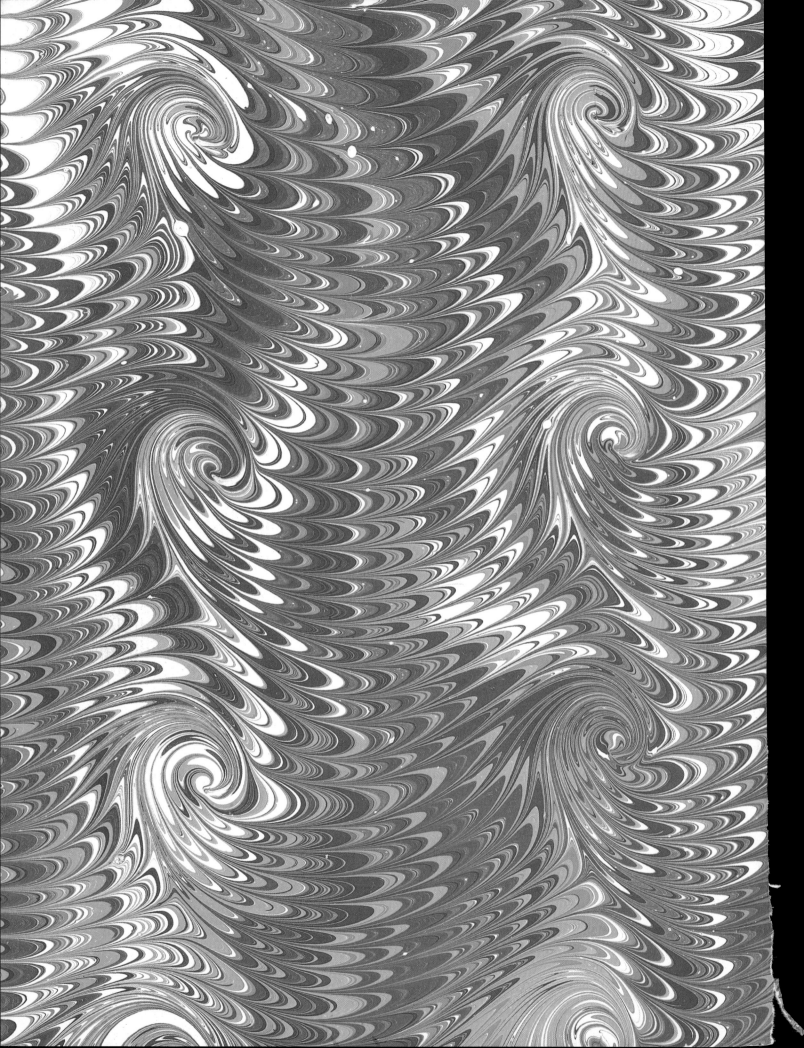